Classic
CAKE DECORATING

Classic
CAKE DECORATING

Rosemary Wadey • Carole Handslip

First published in Great Britain in 1996 by
Parragon Book Service Ltd
Unit 13–17
Avonbridge Trading Estate
Atlantic Road
Avonmouth
Bristol BS11 9QD

ISBN: 0-7525-1607-8

Printed in Italy

Produced by Haldane Mason, London

Acknowledgements
Art Direction: Ron Samuels
Editor: Lisa Dyer
Design: Digital Artworks Partnership Ltd
Photography: Iain Bagwell and Joff Lee
Home Economists: Rosemary Wadey and Carole Handslip

Material in this book has only previously appeared in *Classic Cakes
and Children's Party Cakes*.

Note
Cup measurements in this book are for American cups.
Tablespoons are assumed to be 15ml. Unless otherwise stated, milk is assumed to be
full-fat, eggs are standard size 3 and pepper is freshly ground black pepper.

CONTENTS

INTRODUCTION

Successful cake making and decorating is a very rewarding art that is easily mastered. This book sets out to explain the secrets of baking cakes and icing them, from a simple sponge cake to an elaborate wedding cake.

If you are a beginner, it is important to start with basic techniques and recipes. The book begins with a guide to the equipment need for baking and decorating cakes, instructions on how to line a cake tin (pan) and invaluable charts on adapting ingredients to make cakes of different sizes, as well as lots of ideas for classic cakes such as Carrot Cake and Black Forest Gâteau. Each recipe is fully illustrated and has clear step-by-step instructions.

To help you decorate cakes, there is information on icing equipment, how to cover cakes, how to make decorations such as crystallized flowers and chocolate scrolls, and basic recipes and techniques from simple feathering to piping and making moulded animals and flowers. The recipes include simple ideas that are suitable for any beginner, such as Playing-Card Cake and several gâteaux. For the more experienced cake-maker there are many exciting ideas for both children's party cakes and stunning wedding and celebration cakes. Traditional or modern, simple or elaborate, there is something here for everyone, and whatever you try you will produce successful results every time.

BAKING EQUIPMENT

BEFORE YOU BEGIN baking it is a good idea to check that you have the basic items of equipment. Many of these will already be in your kitchen, but if you have to buy items such as cake tins (pans), it really is worthwhile investing in good-quality ones that will last many years and help give perfect results. Most equipment is available from large department stores and speciality kitchenware shops.

(jelly) roll tins (pans) can be used for biscuits (cookies) and sponge rolls. Loaf tins (pans), for making bread, are also used for fruit or plain cakes. Both the 450 g (1 lb) and 900 g (2 lb) sizes are good to have. Tube or ring moulds are available in many sizes, but the 23 cm (9 inch) size is probably the most versatile. Flan tins (pans) come in sizes for large tarts or small individual tartlets, and may be plain, fluted or in special shapes.

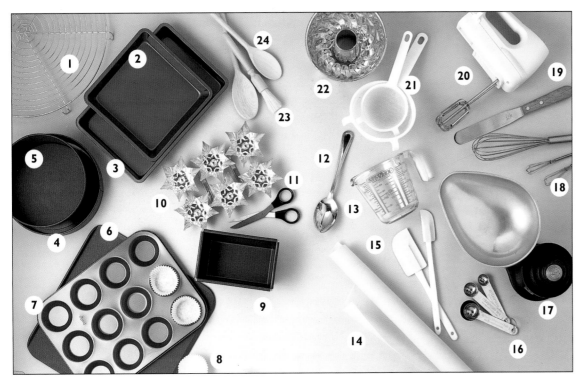

1 Wire cooling rack
2 Square sandwich tin (layer pan) 3 Swiss (jelly) roll tin (pan) 4 Round sandwich tin (layer pan)
5 Deep cake tin (pan)
6 Baking sheet
7 Patty tin (muffin pan)
8 Paper cases
9 Loaf tin (pan)
10 Flan tin (pan)
11 Kitchen scissors
12 Metal spoon
13 Measuring jug 14 Baking parchment 15 Spatulas
16 Measuring spoons
17 Kitchen scales
18 Wire whisks
19 Palette knife (spatula)
20 Electric hand beater
21 Sieves 22 Ring mould
23 Pastry brush
24 Wooden spoons

WEIGHING AND MEASURING TOOLS

There are many types of kitchen scales available, but whichever one you use must be accurate to produce good results. Traditional balance scales are reliable and accurate, but electronic, battery-driven scales are probably the easiest to use.

You will also need a set of metal or plastic measuring spoons and a measuring jug for liquids.

CAKE TINS (PANS)

It is a good idea to have a selection of cake tins (pans) in various shapes and sizes. A non-stick finish is practical, especially for smaller tins (pans) that do not always need lining. To begin with, two round sandwich tins (layer pans) of 20–23 cm (8–9 inches), a deeper round cake tin (pan), a square 5 cm (2 inch) deep cake tin (pan), a Swiss (jelly) roll tin (pan), a flat baking sheet and a patty tin (muffin pan) will be enough.

Sandwich tins (layer pans) should always be bought in pairs and the best size to have is 18 cm (7 inch) or 20 cm (8 inch). Deep cake tins (pans), either round or square, are used for fruit cakes and gingerbread, and the loose-bottomed type are best. Springform pans, which allow the side of the tin to be removed, are useful for gâteaux and cheesecakes. Swiss

Always use the size of tin (pan) stated in the recipe. A tin (pan) that is too big will give a shallow cake that cooks too quickly, and one that is too small will lead to uneven cooking. Tins (pans) with straight rather than sloping sides give the best shape, especially for decorating. Unusually shaped cake tins (pans) can often be hired from specialist shops.

OTHER EQUIPMENT

For mixing, creaming, whisking and beating you will need wooden spoons, a wire balloon whisk and small whisks, spatulas and, to make things a little easier, an electric hand beater. You will also need mixing bowls in different sizes.

Large and small nylon sieves with hooks so they can sit over a bowl are best for sifting flour and icing sugar, but they can also be used for sieving (straining) fruit and jam. A palette knife (spatula) is used for spreading cake mixture into a tin (pan) and smoothing the surface, loosening the sides of a cooked cake, and spreading jam and icing. A dry pastry brush is handy for gently brushing excess crumbs from a cake before icing. Fine skewers, sometimes sold as cake-testers, are essential to judge whether a cake is cooked in the centre. Wire cooling racks should be slightly larger than the size of the cake, so have a round one and an oblong one to hand.

ICING EQUIPMENT

CAKE DECORATING, like all crafts, does require special equipment, but you can start with just a few simple tools and gradually build up your supplies as your skills improve. Equipment used for cake decorating should always be carefully washed and dried after use. Store them carefully, as some nozzles (tips) and cutters are quite fragile and can easily be distorted if just stored freely in a drawer.

CAKE BOARDS AND TURNTABLES

Boards are usually silver or gold, and come in a vast array of sizes and shapes and either thick or thin. It is easy to glue sticky-backed plastic, greaseproof paper or coloured foil on to the cake drum. Cake boards can also be 'banded' to tie in with a design. Choose ribbon of a suitable width and glue around the edge of the board. A cake board should be 5 cm (2 inches) larger than the size of the finished cake. For wedding cakes, the bottom tier should have a board that is 7.5 cm (3 inches) larger than the cake, and no board should be bigger than the cake below it in the tier.

Turntables are usually quite expensive and are only necessary for delicate icing work. For the beginner, just stand the cake on an upturned plate, smaller than the board.

ROLLERS AND SMOOTHERS

A long heavy rolling pin is needed for rolling out marzipan and sugarpaste. A small non-stick rolling pin and board is useful for making small decorations. Spacers are strips of wood or metal that are placed either side of the marzipan or icing when rolling out, to ensure a perfectly even thickness.

When putting marzipan or sugarpaste on to a cake, you need to smooth the surface. Some people like to use their hands, or a rolling pin for the top and a straight-sided jar for the sides. If you want a professional finish, then a plastic smoother with a handle is best to use; they produce very sharp corners on square cakes. To obtain a smooth finish on royal iced cakes, a long plastic or metal scraper is needed for the top. Smaller scrapers can be purchased for the sides and these can be plain, or notched to produce a sculpted edge.

Straight-handled and crank-handled palette knives are useful for spreading, lifting, smoothing and trimming icing.

PIPING TUBES AND BAGS

There is a bewildering array of piping tubes and bags available. To begin, a couple of medium-size piping bags and a few straight line writing tubes (very fine to large, size 00 to 4) and star nozzles (tips) should be enough to pipe messages and simple decorations on most cakes. There are also nozzles (tips) that give different effects, from leaves to animal 'fur'. Nickel-plated plastic nozzles (tips) are more defined than plastic, but also more expensive. Never let icing dry in the nozzles (tips) and as soon as you have finished, put them in a small bowl of warm water and gently clean with a brush.

CUTTING TOOLS AND CUTTERS

A long sharp knife is good for cutting a straight line in marzipan or sugarpaste. A pizza cutter is useful for trimming excess icing from the base of a round cake. A small pointed knife or scalpel is good for cutting out tiny shapes.

1 Decorative beadings
2 Palette knife 3 Plastic cutters 4 Non-edible purchased decorations
5 Food colourings 6 Flower nails 7 Potato peeler
8 Artist's paint brushes
9 Heart-shaped cutters
10 Piping bag and nozzles
11 Tape measure
12 Wooden skewers
13 Sugar thermometer
14 Cake tester 15 Piping bags
16 Cake boards 17 Top smoother 18 Ribbon
19 and 20 Side smoothers
21 Cake band 22 Edible cake decorations 23 Icing moulds
24 Icing sugar shaker
25 Pillars 26 Small cutters

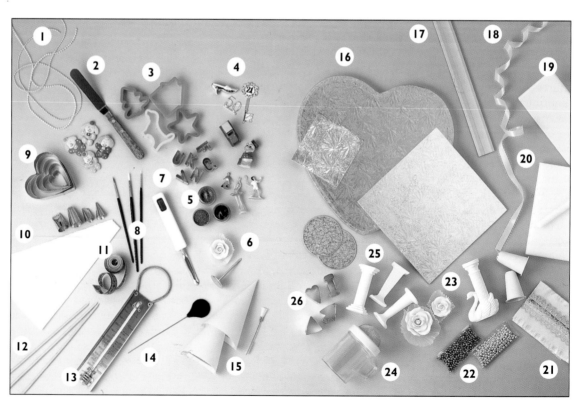

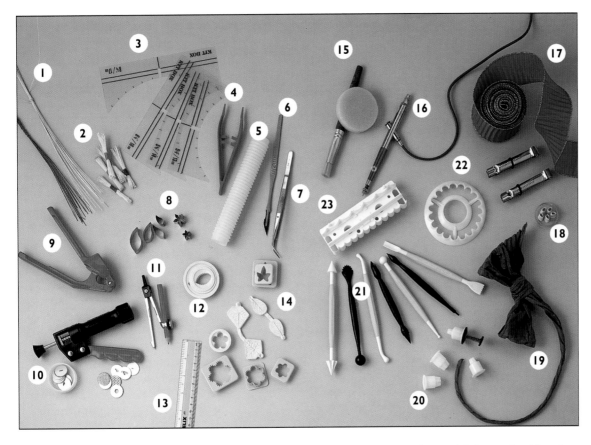

1 Florist's wire 2 Stamens
3 Scrapers 4 Smocking
tweezers 5 Smocking set
6 Scalpel 7 Crimpers 8 Small
cutters 9 Garlic press
10 Extruder 11 Compass
12 Cutters 13 Ruler 14 Icing
moulds 15 Stencilling brush
16 Airbrush 17 Ribbon
18 Cutters 19 Florist's tape
20 Plunger and blossom
cutters 21 Modelling tools
22 Cutter 23 Garrett Frill
cutter

Large stainless steel cutters can be used for plaques and cut-outs and smaller ones are available in flower, letter and number shapes and many more. There are also some specialist cutters, such as the Garrett Frill cutter, which is used for cutting out frills and flounces from icing. Blossom cutters attach to a plunger and when the icing has been cut, the plunger pushes out a pretty flower shape; the icing should be pushed out on to foam to give a good shape.

MODELLING AND SHAPING TOOLS

There are a few household items that can be used for modelling features or shaping icing – round and flat skewers, both ends of a knitting needle, teaspoon handles and so on. But for a more professional finish it is best to buy a set of modelling tools. These can be bought from specialist cake shops or you may be able to find clay modelling tools in a craft shop.

Crimpers are like flat metal tweezers and they are used for making decorative edgings or patterns by gently pinching icing together. Embossing tools, usually plastic, have an embossed pattern on the end which is pressed into the icing.

A smocking set consists of a small ridged rolling pin and tweezers. The icing is rolled out with the rolling pin to create ridges, and the ridges are then pinched together with the tweezer. Tweezers are also useful for positioning tiny decorations; buy a pair with fine points and grooved ends.

FOOD COLOURINGS

There are several types of food colourings available – liquid, paste, powders and pens. Liquid colours are widely available, but are not very concentrated; although they can be used for glacé icing, they will only give a pastel shade to sugarpaste and royal icing. Liquid colours can be applied with an artist's sable paintbrush to paint a design on to the icing.

Paste colours are the best to use for royal icing, sugarpaste and marzipan. They are concentrated so deep colours can be obtained, but should be used sparingly.

Powder food colours are good to use for lace or filigree work because the icing remains stiffer, whereas the glycerine content of pastes will soften the icing. Generally, powder colours are brushed on to flowers and frills. Colour pens are also available, which are like felt-tips and used in the same way to mark out designs or messages. An airbrush can be used with food colours to create dappled and shaded effects.

MISCELLANEOUS TOOLS

A potato peeler is handy for making chocolate curls. Flower nails, available in metal or plastic, are flat or cupped supports on which flowers are piped. A garlic press can be used to create long strands of icing for hair, grass and other effects. An extruder does the same job but you have a choice of discs to fit on the end which give different shapes.

PURCHASED DECORATIONS

Specialist cake decorating shops sell many different types of edible cake decorations, such as sugar flowers, gold and silver dragees, animals, people or numbers.

Non-edible decorations can also be purchased. Stamens for flower decorations are tiny pieces of stiffened thread with a small ball at each end. They are cut in half and pushed into the centre of a moulded flower before it has set. They must be removed from the cake before serving. Florist's wire and tape can also be used to wire flowers to cakes.

PREPARING CAKE TINS (PANS)

Whereas baking cakes that are to be decorated, it is important to make sure they have a firm, even shape and smooth finish. To achieve this, it is essential to use good-quality tins (pans) and to line them.

LINING PAPER

The paper for lining a tin (pan) should be baking parchment or non-stick silicone baking paper. Non-stick paper does not need greasing, but if you use another type, grease it with melted butter or vegetable shortening, or oil it with a mild-flavoured vegetable oil such as sunflower oil. Use a pastry brush to apply a very thin even coat. It is best if the lining is a double thickness to give better insulation and make it easier to remove. The paper must be fitted well into the tin (pan), especially in the corners, to give a smooth edge.

Whether you are using a round, oval, square, hexagonal, heart-shaped or any other type of tin (pan), you only need to know two easy techniques for shaping the lining paper.

LINING A ROUND TIN (PAN)

1 Place the cake tin (pan) on a double thickness of the paper. With a pencil, draw a circle around the base. Cut out the circle just inside (about 5 mm/¼ inch) the marked line to allow for the thickness of the tin and avoid the mark.

2 To line the sides of the tin (pan) you need to measure the circumference. Use a piece of string or a tape measure, or estimate the length by multiplying the diameter by three. Add 5 cm (2 inches) to the length. The width of the strip should be the depth of the tin (pan) plus 5 cm (2 inches). Mark the length and width on the paper and cut out.

3 Fold up one long side of the strip by 2.5 cm (1 inch). Snip at 1 cm (½ inch) intervals, cutting up to the fold. This will allow the paper to curve around the base.

4 Press the strip around the inside of the tin (pan) so that the snipped edge curves neatly around the base and the lining fits snugly. Put in the circle that has been cut for the base and lightly grease if necessary.

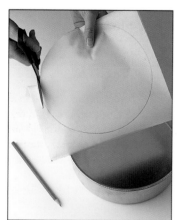

LINING A SQUARE CAKE TIN (PAN)

1 Place the cake tin (pan) on a double thickness of paper. Use a pencil to draw around the base. Cut out the shape just inside (about 5 mm/¼ inch) the marked line to allow for the thickness of the tin (pan) and avoid the mark.

2 Place the tin (pan) on its side on a strip of paper and make a mark on the paper at each corner. Roll the tin (pan) over on to the next side and mark again. Repeat twice more until the length of the tin (pan) and all the corners have been marked on the paper. Add 5 cm (2 inches) on to the strip for overlap. The width of the strip should be the depth of the tin (pan) plus 5 cm (2 inches). Mark on the paper and cut out the strip.

3 Fold up one long side of the strip to a depth of 2.5 cm (1 inch). Then fold the strip widthways where each corner has been marked, so there is a sharp crease for each corner.

4 Open out the strip and snip the folded paper on either side of the corners. With a straight-sided tin (pan), you only have to snip the folded edge at the corners, not all the way along.

5 Press the strip around the inside edge of the tin (pan) so it fits neatly into each corner. Put in the paper that has been cut for the base and lightly grease if necessary. This technique can be used for a straight-sided tin with a number of sides, as long as you fold the paper and snip it at every corner.

LINING A PUDDING BASIN OR BOWL

A pudding basin or bowl may be used to produce a dome-shaped cake. To ensure that the cake turns out cleanly, line the base. Cut out a circle of paper about 5 cm (2 inches) larger than the base of the bowl. Make 5 cm (2 inch) cuts into the circle all the way round. Press the paper into the bowl so the snipped edges overlap and the paper fits snugly in the base. Grease the paper and the sides of the bowl.

SHAPING CAKES

A VARIETY OF DIFFERENT-SHAPED cake tins (pans) can be bought or hired from specialist shops, but with a little ingenuity you can create any number of shapes from cooked cakes without having to purchase a special tin (pan). Many unusual shapes can be formed by breaking down the desired shape into its basic components; for example, an open book is made from two rectangles whose sides are trimmed to make a bevelled edge. Alternatively, the shape can be carved from a single slab. A heart shape, for instance, can be cut from a round cake. Unusual shapes can be created by cooking the cake mixture in containers such as cans. For example, you could make a hamburger novelty cake which has a can of cola at the side: bake some of the mixture in a cleaned-out baked bean can and then ice it to look like a can of cola.

Sometimes it is easier to make a couple of cakes in different shapes, place one on top of the other and then carve out the required shape. This is a good technique for teddy bear and bottle shapes.

CUTTING AND TRIMMING CAKES

For easy cutting or carving, always use a firm-textured cake such as fruit or madeira. A lighter sponge cake will not keep its shape and is harder to manipulate. Most cakes that are to be cut in shapes also need to be covered in marzipan before icing and a lighter sponge would not take the weight of marzipan. It is also best to leave the cake to 'settle' for 12–24 hours before shaping and decorating.

If you intend to layer the cake before carving, then don't be too generous with the filling as it will simply ooze out and the layers will slide around. Use a thin layer of jam or stiff butter cream, just enough to stick the layers together.

A large ham knife is good for slicing cakes horizontally and a small serrated knife is best for trimming and carving smaller details. Always use a sawing motion when carving and brush any crumbs off the cake. If you cut off too much cake by mistake, either stick the piece back on with jam or replace it with marzipan.

BASIC RECIPES

THE FOLLOWING RECIPES HAVE been used for all the cakes throughout the book. The type of cake you make must suit the design and decoration. For instance, if it is to be cut and shaped, the cake should be fairly firm and here a Madeira (Pound) Cake is best, as it keeps its shape and moistness and is easy to coat in butter cream or sugarpaste. Quick Mix Cakes can be used widely too, but the Victoria Sandwich (Sponge Layer) Cake has a much softer texture and is best for a cake without too much sculpture involved. Whatever basic cake recipe you choose, you should leave it to rest on a wire rack with the lining paper attached for 12–24 hours before cutting or decorating. For adapting these recipes to different sizes of cake, see the charts on pages 13–14.

QUICK MIX CAKE

Makes a 30 × 25 cm /12 × 10 inch cake

350 g/12 oz/1½ cups soft margarine
350 g/12 oz/ 1½ cups caster (superfine) sugar
6 eggs
350 g/12 oz/3 cups self-raising flour, sifted
few drops of vanilla flavouring (extract)
3 tsp baking powder

1 Grease and line a rectangular cake tin (pan) , about 30 × 25 cm/ 12 × 10 inches, with baking parchment, as described on page 10.

2 Put the margarine, sugar, eggs, flour, vanilla and baking powder into a bowl and beat vigorously for 2 minutes, either by hand, using a hand-held electric mixer or in a large free-standing mixer.

3 Spread the cake mixture evenly into the prepared tin (pan), level the top and make sure there is plenty of mixture in the corners. Bake in a preheated oven at 180°C/350°F/Gas Mark 4 for about 1–1¼ hours until well risen and firm to the touch. Invert carefully on a wire rack and leave to cool.

VICTORIA SANDWICH (SPONGE LAYER CAKE)

Makes a 30 × 25 cm/12 × 10 inch cake

350 g/12 oz/1½ cups butter or margarine
350 g/12 oz/1½ cups caster (superfine) sugar
6 eggs
350 g/12 oz/3 cups self-raising flour, sifted
2 tbsp water
few drops of vanilla flavouring (extract)

1 Grease and line a rectangular cake tin (pan), about 30 × 25 cm/ 12 × 10 inches, with baking parchment, as described on page 10.

2 Cream the butter and sugar together until light, fluffy and pale. Beat in the eggs one at a time, following each with a tablespoonful of the flour. Fold in the remaining flour, the water and vanilla.

3 Spread the cake mixture evenly intothe prepared tin (pan), level the top aand make sure there is plenty of mixture in the corners. Bake in a preheated oven at 180°C/350°F/Gas Mark 4 for about 50–60 minutes until well risen and firm to the touch. Invert carefully on a wire rack and leave to cool.

Orange or Lemon variation for Victoria Sandwich and Quick Mix cakes: Omit the vanilla and add 1 teaspoon finely grated orange or lemon rind for each egg used in the mixture.

Chocolate variation: Add 2 tablespoons sifted cocoa powder for the 3-egg mixture, 2½ tablespoons for a 4-egg mixture and so on, adding a further ½ tablespoon for each additional egg used in the mixture.

Coffee variation: Add 1 tablespoon instant coffee powder for a 3–4 egg mixture, 1½ tablespoons for a 4-egg mixture and so on, adding a further ½ tablespoon for each additional egg used in the mixture.

MADEIRA (POUND) CAKE

Makes a 23 cm /9 inch deep round or square cake, or a 25 cm /10 inch shallow round or square cake.

300 g/10 oz/1¼ cups butter or margarine
300 g/10 oz/1¼ cups caster (superfine) sugar
5 eggs
300 g/10 oz/2½ cups self-raising flour
150 g/5 oz/1¼ cups plain (all-purpose) flour
grated rind of 2 large lemons
2 tbsp lemon juice

1 Grease and line a deep 23 cm/9 inch, or a shallow 25 cm/10 inch, round or square cake tin (pan) with baking parchment, as described on page 10.

2 Cream the butter or margarine and caster (superfine) sugar together until very light, fluffy and pale in colour. Then beat in the eggs one at a time, following each with a tablespoonful of the flour.

3 Sift the remaining flours together and fold them into the creamed mixture, followed by the lemon rind and juice. Spoon

into the prepared tin (pan) and level the top, making sure there is plenty of mixture in the corners.

4 Bake in a preheated oven at 160°C/325°F/Gas Mark 3 for about 1¼–1½ hours for the 25 cm/10 inch tin (pan); or about 1¼–1¼ hours for the 23 cm /9 inch tin (pan), until the cake is well risen, golden brown and firm to the touch. Cool in the tin (pan) for a few minutes, then invert on a wire rack and leave to cool.

Coffee variation: Omit the lemon rind and juice and replace the lemon juice quantity with coffee essence.

Chocolate variation: Omit the lemon rind and juice and replace the lemon juice quantity with water. Add 1 tablespoon sifted cocoa powder for a 2-egg cake, add 1½ tablespoons for a 3-egg cake and so on, adding a further ½ tablespoon for each additional egg used in the mixture.

RICH FRUIT CAKE

Makes a 20 cm (8 inch) square cake.

275 g/9 oz/2¼ cups plain (all-purpose) flour
1½ tsp ground mixed spice
½ tsp ground nutmeg
250 g/8 oz/1 cup butter or margarine
250 g/8 oz/1⅓ cups soft brown sugar
grated rind of 1 lemon
1 tbsp black treacle (molasses)
5 large eggs
350 g/12 oz/2 cups currants
250 g/8 oz/1⅓ cups sultanas (golden raisins)
175 g/6 oz/1 cup raisins
125 g/4 oz/½ cup glacé (candied) cherries, chopped
90 g/3 oz/½ cup cut mixed (candied) peel or chopped dates
90 g/3 oz/¾ cup ground almonds
90 g/3 oz/½ cup blanched almonds, chopped

1 Prepare a 20 cm/8 inch square deep cake tin (pan) as described on page 10.

2 Sift the flour, mixed spice and nutmeg together in a bowl.

3 Cream the butter or margarine and sugar together with the lemon rind until light and fluffy, then mix in the black treacle (molasses).

4 Beat in the eggs one at a time, adding a tablespoon of flour with each egg after the first one.

5 Fold in the remaining flour with the fruit and nuts until thoroughly mixed.

6 Turn the mixture into the prepared cake tin (pan) and smooth the top with a palette knife (spatula).

7 Place the cake on a pad of newspaper and bake on the middle shelf of a preheated oven at 170°C/325°F/Gas Mark 3 for 1 hour. Reduce to 150°C/300°F/Gas Mark 2 and bake for a further 2–3 hours. When a skewer inserted into the centre of the cake comes out clean, it is cooked. Leave in the tin (pan) for 30 minutes before turning on to a wire rack to cool.

CAKE CHARTS

SPONGE CAKE CHART

Square tin (pan)	12 cm 5 inch	15 cm 6 inch	18 cm 7 inch	20 cm 8 inch	23 cm 9 inch	25 cm 10 inch	28 cm 11 inch
Round tin (pan)	15 cm 6 inch	18 cm 7 inch	20 cm 8 inch	23 cm 9 inch	25 cm 10 inch	28 cm 11 inch	30 cm 12 inch
Butter or margarine	60 g 2 oz	125 g 4 oz	175 g 6 oz	250 g 8 oz	350 g 12 oz	475 g 15 oz	500 g 1 lb
Caster (superfine) sugar	60 g 2 oz	125 g 4 oz	175 g 6 oz	250 g 8 oz	350 g 12 oz	475 g 15 oz	500 g 1 lb
Eggs	1	2	3	4	6	8	9
Self-raising flour	60 g 2 oz	125 g 4 oz	175 g 6 oz	250 g 8 oz	350 g 12 oz	475 g 15 oz	500 g 1 lb
Approx. cooking time	20–30 mins	30–40 mins	40–50 mins	1 hour	1¼ hours	1½ hours	1¾ hours

Oven temperature: 160°C/325°F/Gas Mark 3

MADEIRA (POUND) CAKE CHART

Square tin (pan)	15 cm 6 inch	18 cm 7 inch	20 cm 8 inch	23 cm 9 inch	25 cm 10 inch	28 cm 11inch
Round tin (pan)	18 cm 7 inch	20 cm 8 inch	23 cm 9 inch	25 cm 10 inch	28 cm 11 inch	30 cm 12 inch
Plain (all-purpose) flour	250 g 8 oz	350 g 12 oz	475 g 15 oz	500 g 1 lb	625 g 1¼ lb	750 g 1½ lb
Baking powder	1 tsp	1½ tsp	2 tsp	2½ tsp	3 tsp	3½ tsp
Caster (superfine) sugar	175 g 6 oz	300 g 10 oz	425 g 14 oz	475 g 15 oz	500 g 1 lb	675 g 1 lb 6 oz
Butter or margarine	175 g 6 oz	300 g 10 oz	425 g 14 oz	475 g 15 oz	500 g 1 lb	675 g 1 lb 6 oz
Eggs	3	5	7	8	10	12
Milk	2 tbsp	3 tbsp	3½ tbsp	4 tbsp	4½ tbsp	5 tbsp
Approx. cooking time	1¼–1½ hours	1½–1¾ hours	1¾–2 hours	1¾–2 hours	2–2¼ hours	2¼–2½ hours

Oven temperature: 160°C/325°F/Gas Mark 3

RICH FRUIT CAKE CHART

Square tin (pan)	12 cm 5 inch	15 cm 6 inch	18 cm 7 inch	20 cm 8 inch	23 cm 9 inch	25 cm 10 inch
Round tin (pan)	15 cm 6 inch	18 cm 7 inch	20 cm 8 inch	23 cm 9 inch	25 cm 10 inch	28 cm 11 inch
Mixed dried fruit	425 g 14 oz	625 g 1¼ lb	850 g 1 lb 12 oz	1 kg 2 lb	1.5 kg 3 lb	1.75 kg 3½ lb
Chopped glacé (candied) cherries	60 g 2 oz	90 g 3 oz	150 g 5 oz	175 g 6 oz	275 g 9 oz	300 g 10 oz
Chopped nuts	30 g 1 oz	60 g 2 oz	90 g 3 oz	125 g 4 oz	150 g 5 oz	200 g 7 oz
Mixed (candied) peel	30 g 1 oz	60 g 2 oz	90 g 3 oz	125 g 4 oz	150 g 5 oz	200 g 7 oz
Grated lemon rind	1 tsp	1½ tsp	2 tsp	2½ tsp	3 tsp	3½ tsp
Brandy or rum	1 tbsp	1 tbsp	1½ tbsp	2 tbsp	2½ tbsp	3 tbsp
Butter or margarine	150 g 5 oz	175 g 6 oz	300 g 10 oz	350 g 12 oz	500 g 1 lb	625 g 1¼ lb
Soft brown sugar	150 g 5 oz	175 g 6 oz	275 g 10 oz	350 g 12 oz	500 g 1 lb	600 g 1¼ lb
Eggs	2	3	5	6	8	9
Plain (all-purpose) flour	200 g 7 oz	250 g 8 oz	350 g 12 oz	425 g 14 oz	625 g 1¼ lb	675 g 1 lb 6 oz
Ground mixed spice	½ tsp	1 tsp	1½ tsp	2 tsp	2½ tsp	3 tsp
Approx. cooking time	2–2¼ hours	2¼–2½ hours	2½–2¾ hours	3–3½ hours	3½–3¾ hours	4–4½ hours

Oven temperature: 140°C/275°F/Gas Mark 1

BASIC QUICK MIX SPONGE CHART FOR UNUSUAL SIZES

Tin (pan) size	2 × 18 cm (7 inch) sandwich (layer) tins (pans)	2 × 20 cm (8 inch) sandwich (layer) tins (pans)	18 paper cake cases or patty (muffin) tins	900 ml/1½ pint /3¾ cup pudding basin	1 litre/1¾ pint /4 cup pudding basin	28 × 18 × 4 cm /11 × 7 × 1½ inch slab cake
Soft margarine	125 g 4 oz	175 g 6 oz	125 g 4 oz	125 g 4 oz	175 g 6 oz	175 g 6 oz
Caster (superfine) sugar	125 g 4 oz	175 g 6 oz	125 g 4 oz	125 g 4 oz	175 g 6 oz	175 g 6 oz
Eggs, size 1 or 2	2	3	2	2	3	3
Self-raising flour	125 g 4 oz	175 g 6 oz	125 g 4 oz	125 g 4 oz	175 g 6 oz	175 g 6 oz
Baking powder	1 tsp	1½ tsp	1 tsp	1 tsp	1½ tsp	1½ tsp
Approx. cooking time	25–30 mins	30–35 mins	15–20 mins	50 mins	1 hour	30–40 mins

Oven temperature: 160°C/325°F/Gas Mark 3

ICINGS (FROSTINGS) & DECORATIONS

The icings (frostings) and cake decorations on the following pages cover the entire range of cake decoration, from simple coverings to elaborate piping and moulding. Glacé icing (frosting) is probably the simplest cake covering and can be poured over a sponge cake. Butter icing (frosting) is also very easy to make and an attractive result can be achieved by marking it with a fork or palette knife (spatula) to make a swirled effect. Chocolate fudge icing (frosting), chocolate ganache and butter cream take a little more time to prepare, though they are all relatively easy for a beginner and all can be used on sponge cakes. There are also recipes for sugarpaste, marzipan and royal icing, probably the most versatile and popular cake coverings. Many variations for adding different flavourings to the icings (frostings), such as lemon or coffee, are also given throughout the chapter. For creating more ornate decorations, there are detailed instructions on how to make curls, leaves, dipped fruit and carved shapes from chocolate. There are ideas for piping and moulding with royal icing and sugarpaste to enable you to decorate your cakes with everything from intricate piped trellises and lettering to pretty flowers and amusing animals.

Marzipan & Apricot Glaze (page 28)

Glacé & Feather Icing (Frosting)

Glacé icing (frosting) is a very quickly made water icing (frosting), used to cover the top of a cake. It consists of sugar and water, making it a good choice for beginners. Feather icing (frosting) is one of the decorative techniques for which glacé icing (frosting) can be used.

Information	Equipment
Covers a 23 cm/9 inch cake	mixing bowl and spoon
Level of Difficulty: ☆	piping bag
Storage: use immediately	small writing nozzle (tip)
	palette knife (spatula)

GLACÉ ICING (FROSTING)

1 Sift the icing (confectioners') sugar into a bowl and add 1–2 tablespoons water gradually.

2 The icing (frosting) is the right consistency when it coats the back of a spoon thickly.

3 Add the flavouring or colouring and use immediately.

Step 1 – *Glacé Icing*

Step 2 – *Glacé Icing*

INGREDIENTS

Glacé Icing (Frosting)

250 g/8 oz/2 cups icing (confectioners') sugar

flavouring or food colouring

Feather Icing (Frosting)

1 quantity glacé icing (frosting)

food colouring

GLACE ICING (FROSTING) VARIATIONS

Coffee: Replace 1 tablespoon water with coffee flavouring (extract).

Orange or Lemon: Replace 1 tablespoon water with orange or lemon juice and add the grated rind of 1 orange or lemon.

Chocolate: Sift 1 tablespoon cocoa powder with the icing (confectioners') sugar.

FEATHER ICING (FROSTING)

1 Place a quarter of the icing (frosting) in a bowl, add a few drops of food colouring and mix thoroughly.

2 Spoon the coloured icing (frosting) into a piping bag fitted with a No. 1 writing nozzle (tip) and fold over the top.

3 Put the cake on a wire rack and pour on the remaining uncoloured icing (frosting).

Step 4 – *Feather Icing*

Step 5 – *Feather Icing*

4 Spread almost to the edge with a small palette knife (spatula) and give a couple of sharp taps on the cake board or plate so that the icing (frosting) flows smoothly to the edge.

5 Using the coloured icing (frosting), pipe a continuous spiral on top of the cake, keeping the lines 1 cm/½ inch apart. Working quickly, pull the point of a small knife across the lines from the edge to the centre and back several times to make a feather pattern.

Butter Cream &
Butter Icing (Frosting)

Both of these are very light and creamy-textured icings (frostings)
suitable for covering the top and sides of a cake and filling the
centre. Butter cream is often referred to as crème au beurre.

Information	Equipment
Both fill and cover a 20 cm/8 inch cake	saucepan
Level of Difficulty: ✷	mixing bowl and spoons
Storage: use immediately	electric beater or whisk

BUTTER CREAM

1 Put the egg whites and sugar into a mixing bowl over a saucepan of simmering water and whisk until the mixture holds its shape. Leave to cool slightly.

2 Beat the butter until soft and creamy, then whisk in the meringue mixture gradually. Flavour and colour as liked.

INGREDIENTS

Butter Cream

2 egg whites

125 g/4 oz/1 cup icing (confectioners') sugar, sifted

125 g/4 oz/½ cup butter

flavouring or food colouring

Butter Icing (Frosting)

125 g/4 oz/½ cup softened butter

250 g/8 oz/2 cups icing (confectioners') sugar, sifted

1–2 tbsp milk

flavouring or food colouring

BUTTER ICING (FROSTING)

1 Put the butter into a bowl and beat with a wooden spoon until creamy.

2 Stir in the icing (confectioners') sugar gradually with enough milk to mix to a smooth soft icing (frosting). Flavour and colour as preferred.

Step 1 – Butter Cream

Step 2 – Butter Cream

BUTTER ICING FLAVOURINGS

Orange or lemon: Add the grated rind of 1 fresh orange or lemon to the butter. Replace the milk with the orange or lemon juice. Add a few drops of food colouring.

Chocolate: Blend 2 tablespoons cocoa powder with 2 tablespoons boiling water. Leave to cool, then add with a little milk if necessary.

Coffee: Replace 1 tablespoon milk with coffee flavouring (extract).

BUTTER CREAM FLAVOURINGS

Chocolate or coffee: Add 60 g/2 oz/2 squares of cooled melted chocolate, or 1 tablespoon coffee flavouring (extract), to the finished butter cream.

Step 1 – Butter Icing

Step 2 – Butter Icing

Sugarpaste & Royal Icing

Sugarpaste is extremely pliable and very easy to use both for covering cakes and moulding into decorations; ready-made paste is also available. Royal icing is used for more elaborately decorated rich fruit cakes.

Information	Equipment
Both make 500 g/1 lb	mixing bowls and spoons
Level of Difficulty: ★	
Storage: Royal icing can be stored for 4–5 days and sugarpaste for 3–4 days in airtight containers in the refrigerator.	

Step 1 – *Sugarpaste*

Step 2 – *Sugarpaste*

INGREDIENTS

Sugarpaste

1 egg white

1 tbsp liquid glucose

425 g/15 oz/3¾ cups icing
(confectioners') sugar, sifted

Royal Icing

2 egg whites

500 g/1 lb/4 cups icing
(confectioners') sugar

1 tsp lemon juice

1 tsp glycerine

FLOWERPASTE

Knead 2 teaspoons gum
tragacanth into the sugarpaste.
This will make it more malleable
and easier to use, and especially
good for making fine quality
moulded flowers.

Step 2 – *Royal Icing*

Step 3 – *Royal Icing*

SUGARPASTE

1 Mix the egg white and glucose
together with a fork. Mix in the
icing (confectioners') sugar
gradually with a wooden spoon
until it forms a stiff paste.

2 When the paste becomes too
thick to mix with a spoon,
transfer it to a work surface
(counter) and knead using your
fingers to blend in the icing
(confectioners') sugar.

3 Knead it until smooth,
then wrap it in clingfilm
(plastic wrap).

ROYAL ICING

For flat surfaces or for piping
rosettes and flowers, royal icing
should be fairly firm, but hold soft
peaks. For writing, lattice work or
loops, it should be a little thinner.
This makes enough to cover a
15 cm/6 inch cake with 3 coats and
some simple decoration.

1 Beat the egg whites with a fork
until frothy.

2 Gradually mix in half the sugar
with a wooden spoon.

3 Mix in the lemon juice and
glycerine with enough of the
remaining sugar to give an icing
that stands in soft peaks. It must be
beaten until it is snowy-white.

4 Cover the surface of the icing
with clingfilm (plastic wrap) to
prevent a crust forming.

How to Cover with Sugarpaste

Sugarpaste is one of the most versatile icings (frostings) and is easy to make and use – see pages 20–21 for the recipe. It is a good alternative to royal icing for celebration cakes and extremely useful for novelty cakes.

Information	*Equipment*
Level of Difficulty: ☆	rolling pin
	sharp knife

Step 2

Step 3

Step 4

Step 5

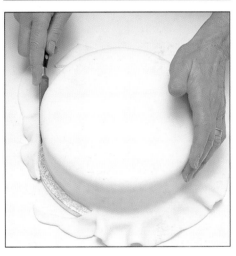

USING SUGARPASTE

Ready-made sugarpaste, sometimes called 'ready to roll' icing (frosting), is very good if you do not have time to make your own. Some varieties, however, are soft and sticky and may need a little extra icing (confectioners') sugar kneaded into them.

If the sugarpaste becomes dry, dip it into hot water, put it into a plastic bag for 1 hour and then knead again. As it is white, it is simple to achieve natural colours. Food colourings, preferably paste, can easily be kneaded into the icing (frosting) or painted on the finished decoration, but do make sure you colour sufficient sugarpaste to finish each project. You can achieve interesting effects by only partially kneading in the colouring, so that when you roll out the icing (frosting), it has a marbled effect.

Attach flowers or other decorations moulded from sugarpaste to the covered cake with egg white or royal icing.

AIR BUBBLES

Try to avoid trapping air under the sugarpaste. If an air bubble does appear, prick with a large pin and smooth the sugarpaste again.

1 Make sure the cake surface is perfectly smooth, as all imperfections will show through. The cake may first be covered with marzipan (see page 29) but should then be brushed with sherry or water, so that the sugarpaste will stick. If using to cover a sponge cake, spread a thin layer of Butter Icing (Frosting) (see pages 18–19) over the cake first and then chill it for 1 hour. Alternatively, brush with Apricot Glaze (see page 29).

2 Roll out the sugarpaste fairly thinly on a work surface (counter) dusted with cornflour (cornstarch) or icing (confectioners') sugar until 10 cm/ 4 inches larger than the cake.

3 Lift the sugarpaste on a rolling pin, lay over the cake and smooth over the top and sides, using hands dusted with cornflour (cornstarch).

4 Ease the sugarpaste around the sides, smoothing gently to remove any creases.

5 Trim off the excess sugarpaste around the base of the cake with a sharp knife.

How to Cover with Royal Icing

Royal icing (see pages 20–21) needs patience and practice, but has a
beautifully smooth, crisp finish. For the best results use a turntable, a
straight edge (a long rigid metal ruler) and a side scraper.

Information	Equipment
Level of Difficulty: ☆	cake board or turntable
	palette knife (spatula)
	metal ruler
	sharp knife
	side scraper

Step 2

4 Place the cake on a turntable and, using a palette knife (spatula), spread some icing around the side of the cake as smoothly and evenly as possible.

Step 4

1 Secure the cake to a cake board or turntable with a little royal icing and leave to dry.

2 Spread some royal icing evenly over the cake top with a paddling movement, using a palette knife (spatula).

3 Draw a long rigid metal ruler, held at a slight angle, across the top of the cake towards you in one continuous movement. Remove the surplus icing with a knife held parallel to the side of the cake and leave to dry.

5 Hold the scraper at a slight angle against the side of the cake and rotate 1 complete turn. Remove the surplus icing from the cake top and base with a palette knife (spatula) and leave to dry for 12 hours. If covering a square cake, coat 2 opposite sides with icing and leave to dry for 12 hours. Then coat the remaining sides.

6 When completely dry, remove any rough edges, using a sharp knife and a clean brush. Apply 2 more coats of thin royal icing in the same way, making sure each coat is completely dry before adding the next. Leave to dry before decorating.

HINTS

Make royal icing to a soft peak consistency 12 hours in advance and cover the bowl with clingfilm (plastic wrap) and a damp cloth to prevent it from drying out. Stir before use to disperse any bubbles. An electric mixer is not recommended, as too much air will be incorporated, causing the icing to be fluffy and full of bubbles.

To ice the cake board, use a small palette knife (spatula) to spread royal icing evenly over the board. Smooth the icing, holding a scraper steady while turning the turntable. Remove the surplus icing on the edge.

Step 3

Step 6

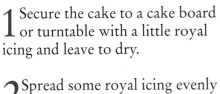

Chocolate Fudge Icing (Frosting) & Chocolate Ganache

These are perfect for chocolate-lovers! Chocolate ganache in particular is perhaps the richest and most irresistible of all icings (frostings) and is especially well suited to covering little cakes and petit fours.

Information	Equipment
Both fill and cover a 20 cm/8 inch cake Level of Difficulty: ✷ ✷	saucepans and spoons

Step 1 – *Chocolate Fudge*

Step 2 – *Chocolate Fudge*

Chocolate Fudge Icing (Frosting)

60 g/2 oz/¼ cup butter

3 tbsp milk

250 g/8 oz/2 cups icing (confectioners') sugar, sifted

2 tbsp sifted cocoa powder

Chocolate Ganache

175 g/6 oz/6 squares dark chocolate, broken into pieces

4 tbsp single (light) cream

60 g/2 oz/¼ cup butter, cut into cubes

2 egg yolks

1 tbsp brandy

Step 1 – *Chocolate Ganache*

Step 2 – *Chocolate Ganache*

CHOCOLATE FUDGE ICING (FROSTING)

A rich mixture that can be used to coat cakes when it is warm, or used as a filling if left to cool and then beaten until soft.

1 Melt the butter in a small saucepan with the milk.

2 Add the sugar and cocoa, and beat well until smooth and glossy.

3 Leave until tepid, then pour over the cake.

VARIATIONS

Coffee Fudge: Replace the cocoa powder with 2 teaspoons instant coffee granules.

White Fudge: Use only 2 tablespoons milk, add 60 g/ 2 oz/2 squares white chocolate to the saucepan and omit the cocoa powder.

CHOCOLATE GANACHE

Used while warm, this will cover a cake thickly, giving a lovely glossy coat. Alternatively, if you want to use it as a filling or for piping, leave it to cool and then beat it thoroughly.

1 Put the chocolate into a small saucepan with the cream and heat gently until melted.

2 Leave to cool slightly, then beat in the butter gradually.

3 Beat in the egg yolks and brandy. Leave to cool slightly until firm, stirring occasionally.

Marzipan & Apricot Glaze

Homemade marzipan, or almond paste as it is sometimes called,
has a wonderful flavour and texture. Brush your cake with apricot
glaze before applying marzipan or sugarpaste.

Information	Equipment
Marzipan makes 750 g/1½ lb/8¼ cups	mixing bowls and spoons
Apricot Glaze makes 250 g/8 oz/3¾ cup	saucepan
Level of Difficulty: ★	sieve (strainer)
Storage: In a refrigerator, the marzipan will keep for 1–2 weeks in a plastic bag; the glaze will keep for 2–3 months in an airtight jar.	

Step 1 – *Marzipan*

Step 2 – *Marzipan*

INGREDIENTS

Marzipan

350 g/12 oz/3 cups
ground almonds

175 g/6 oz/¾ cup caster
(superfine) sugar

175 g/6 oz/1½ cups icing
(confectioners')
sugar, sifted

1 egg, beaten

1 egg yolk

few drops almond flavouring
(extract)

2 tsp lemon juice

Apricot Glaze

250 g/8 oz/¾ cup
apricot jam

2 tbsp water

1 tsp lemon juice

Step 1 – *Apricot Glaze*

Step 2 – *Apricot Glaze*

Marzipan

1 Put the ground almonds into a bowl with the sugars and make a well in the centre. Stir in the beaten egg, egg yolk, almond flavouring (extract) and lemon juice.

2 Mix to a smooth paste. Do not overknead the paste or it will become oily and difficult to handle.

COVERING A CAKE WITH MARZIPAN

Roll out the marzipan to 5 mm/¼ inch thick on a surface (counter) dusted with icing (confectioners') sugar. Cut out a disc or square the same size as the cake top. Brush the top of the cake with apricot glaze, invert the cake on the marzipan, then turn the covered cake over. Brush the sides with the apricot glaze. Roll out the remaining marzipan, cut a long strip, or four strips, to fit around the sides of the cake, dust with sugar and roll or press it round the sides of the cake to cover. Leave to dry for 24 hours at room temperature.

Apricot Glaze

1 Put the apricot jam, water and lemon juice into a small saucepan and heat gently until melted. Bring to the boil and simmer for a few minutes.

2 Sieve (strain) the mixture, then return it to the pan, scraping any jam from the bottom of the sieve (strainer).

3 Heat before using and add a little more water if the glaze is too thick.

Chocolate Decorations

Chocolate can be melted and made into a wide range of
luscious-looking decorations that are really quite easy to achieve.
However, care must be taken when melting chocolate.

Information	Equipment
Level of Difficulty: ★	Saucepan
	heatproof mixing bowl and spoons
	cutters or sharp knife
	piping bag
	small writing nozzle (tip)

Chocolate Shapes

CHOCOLATE SHAPES

1 Spread a thin layer of melted chocolate on to baking parchment and leave until set but not too hard.

2 Cut out shapes with cutters or a sharp knife. Pipe a different colour of chocolate on the shapes to decorate.

DIPPED FRUIT AND NUTS

1 Add 1–2 teaspoons vegetable oil, or more if necessary, to the required quantity of melted chocolate to make it more fluid.

Dipped Fruit

TO MELT CHOCOLATE

Break some chocolate into small pieces and place in a heatproof bowl that fits snugly over a saucepan of water. Bring the water to the boil, turn off the heat and leave until the chocolate has melted. If it is overheated or if any steam or water comes into contact with the chocolate, it will become stiff and granular and lose its smooth glossiness.

Alternatively, put the chocolate in a heatproof bowl and place in a microwave oven at full power for 2 minutes, stirring occasionally.

2 Half-dip fruits such as strawberries, physalis (ground cherries) or grapes, drain off as much chocolate as possible and place on baking parchment to set. Walnuts, almonds and Brazil nuts can also be dipped.

PIPED CHOCOLATE

1 Pour melted chocolate into a baking parchment piping bag and leave to cool slightly so the consistency is not too thin. Snip off the end and pipe zigzag lines.

CHOCOLATE CURLS

1 Scrape a potato peeler across a block of chocolate. The chocolate should not be too cold or the curls will break into small pieces.

Piped Chocolate

GRATED CHOCOLATE

1 Use a coarse grater and make sure the chocolate and your hands are cold. Keep turning the chocolate as you grate.

CHOCOLATE LEAVES

1 Coat one side of clean rose leaves with melted chocolate. Leave to dry. Paint a second coat. When hard, peel the leaf away.

Chocolate Curls

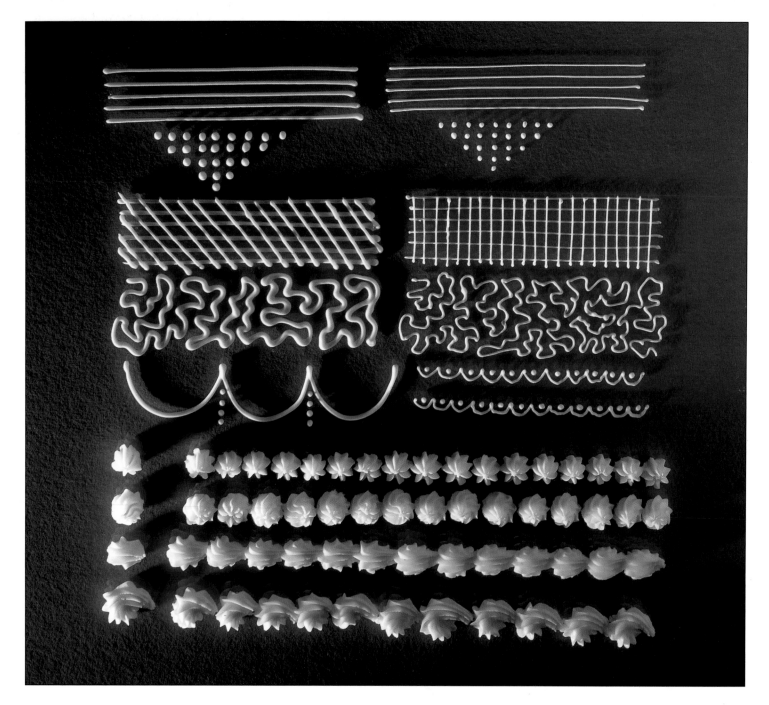

How to Pipe

Practise piping on a flat surface or cake tin (pan). The consistency of the icing must be correct for each type of piping. If the icing is too stiff, it will require too much pressure to squeeze it out; if too thin, the shape will lose its definition. For writing, the icing needs to be a little looser.

Once you get the hang of it, you will become enthralled with this technique and want to experiment further. All you need is imagination and a little spare time.

Information	*Equipment*
Level of Difficulty: ★ ★	piping bags
	assorted nozzles (tips) in various sizes

1 Half-fill a piping bag with Royal Icing (see pages 20–21) and fold over the top to secure. Hold between the first two fingers and thumb of one hand, guide with the other hand, and apply even pressure at the top of the bag.

2 For lines, squeeze out enough icing to touch the surface. Squeezing the bag gently, lift the nozzle (tip) a little and pull it towards you. The icing comes out in a sagging line; manoeuvre it to keep it straight. To finish, touch the surface with the nozzle (tip). Loops can be made on the sides of the cake more easily if it is tilted. Hold the nozzle (tip) away from the

cake and let the icing fall into an even loop.

3 For trellis work, first pipe a series of parallel lines. When dry, pipe another layer of parallel lines in the opposite direction over the first layer. For a more delicate effect, use a finer nozzle (tip) to pipe a third and fourth layer over the top, allowing each layer to dry first.

4 For writing, practise capital letters first, then handwriting. Draw the words on baking parchment and prick through the paper on to the surface of the iced (frosted) cake with a straight pin.

Take off the paper and pipe over the pin marks.

5 For lacework, hold the nozzle (tip) close to the cake and pipe a continuous wiggly line, keeping the spaces and size even.

6 For a star, hold the bag upright just above the cake's surface. Squeeze out the icing, then make a quick down-and-up movement to make a squat star.

7 For a rosette, hold the bag upright just above the cake's surface. Squeeze the icing in a circular movement towards the centre. Curl it into the centre and finish off sharply, leaving a slightly raised central point.

8 For a shell, use a star nozzle (tip). Hold the bag at an angle just above the cake. Squeeze the icing on to the cake until a head is formed. Pull the bag back gently and at the same time release the pressure. The shell will come to a neat point.

9 For a scroll, use a star nozzle (tip). Hold the bag just above the cake. Squeeze out the icing in a comma shape, beginning with a thick head, gradually releasing pressure on the bag while pulling into a long tail. Repeat to form a border.

Step 3

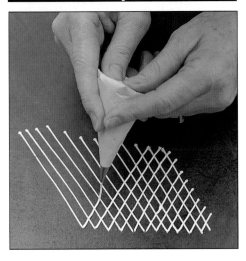

Step 6

Step 4

Step 9

How to Pipe Flowers

To pipe flowers you will need a petal nozzle (tip), an icing nail and some small squares of waxed paper. Petal nozzles (tips) are made in different sizes – large, medium and small. You can make roses, daisies, primroses and daffodils, as well as leaves.

Information	Equipment
Level of Difficulty: ★ ★	piping bags
	petal nozzles (tips) in various sizes
	icing nail
	waxed paper

1 Place a little royal icing (see pages 20–21) on top of the icing nail and stick a square of waxed paper on top.

2 For a rose, hold the piping bag with the thin part of the nozzle (tip) upwards. Pipe a small cone of royal icing, twisting the nail between finger and thumb. Pipe 3–5 overlapping petals around the centre of the rose, allowing the outer petals to curve outwards.

3 For a daisy, work with the thick edge of the nozzle (tip) to the centre and, keeping it flat, pipe 5 small rounded white petals, turning the nail as each petal is being piped. Pipe small dots in the centre to resemble stamens. When dry, paint the edges with pink food colouring.

4 For a primrose, use yellow royal icing and pipe as for the daisy, then pipe a white dot in the centre.

5 For a daffodil, use yellow royal icing and pipe as for the daisy, then leave to dry. Using a small petal nozzle (tip), pipe a trumpet in the centre, twisting the nail quickly to make a complete circle. When dry, paint the edges of the trumpet and petals with a darker yellow food colouring.

6 For leaves, you can use a leaf nozzle (tip) but, for smaller leaves, a piping bag without a nozzle (tip) gives a better effect. Fill the bag, but don't cut off the tip. Press the tip of the bag flat, then snip off the point in the shape of an arrow. Place the tip of the bag on a sheet of waxed paper, holding it at a slight angle. Press out the royal icing and pull away quickly to make a tapering point.
Serrated leaves can be made by moving the nozzle (tip) backwards and forwards.

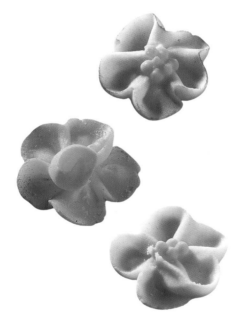

Step 2

Step 4

Step 3

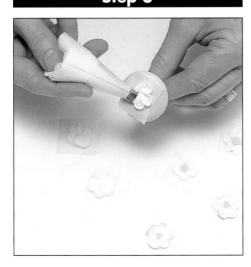

HINTS

Leave the flowers and leaves to dry for 24 hours before removing from the waxed paper. They will keep indefinitely in an airtight container.

When you are more experienced, you can pipe leaves directly on to a cake; they also look pretty piped in white on wedding cakes.

Step 6

How to Mould Flowers & Animals

Sugarpaste is pliable and easy to mould and you can colour the paste to suit the subject. For Royal Icing and Sugarpaste recipes, see pages 20–21.

Information	Equipment
Level of Difficulty: ✯ ✯	carnation and daisy cutters
	cocktail sticks (toothpicks)
	modelling tools
	piping bag and small nozzles (tips)

Roses	Carnations	Daisies

 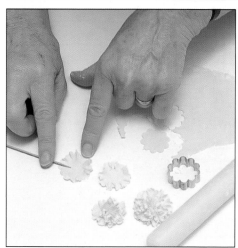 

ROSES

1 Make a cone with a small piece of sugarpaste and press out the base to make a stand. Place upright.

2 Flatten a piece of sugarpaste the size of a pea in the palm of your hand, using cornflour (cornstarch) to prevent it from sticking. Using a cold cooked egg in its shell, flatten one end of the sugarpaste with quick, gentle strokes until it looks like a very thin petal.

3 Moisten the centre of the petal with egg white and wrap around the top of the cone to form a bud. Make another petal and wrap around the bud. Repeat, overlapping each petal until the desired shape is achieved, bending the outside petals over at the top. Leave to dry overnight. Cut off the base and attach to the cake with egg white.

CARNATIONS

1 Roll out a piece of sugarpaste very thinly and cut out 2 discs, using a carnation cutter.

2 Frill the edges of both discs by rolling a cocktail stick (toothpick) gently backwards and forwards. Gather 1 together to form the flower and place it on the other flat frilled disc. Attach with egg white. Repeat with a third and fourth frilled disc and attach them to the first.

DAISIES

1 Roll out some sugarpaste thinly and cut into shapes with a daisy cutter. Place the daisy on a piece of foam sponge, press the centre with a ball modelling tool to give a daisy shape and leave to dry overnight.

2 Brush the tips of the petals with pink confectioners' dusting powder (petal dust/blossom tint) and pipe small yellow dots in the centre with royal icing.

Animals

SNAIL

1 Shape a small piece of green sugarpaste into a sausage wider at one end and pointed at the other. Shape a ball of purple sugarpaste and attach to the green sausage, using egg white.

2 Using red royal icing, pipe circular lines on the purple shell. Pipe eyes on the green head.

GATEAUX & CLASSIC CAKES

In this chapter you will find a selection of ornate gâteaux, such as Black Forest and Chocolate Caraque, which are perfect for special occasions, alongside more classic and 'homey' recipes, such as Carrot Cake and Sherry & Spice Cake. A gâteau makes an elaborate and attractive dinner-party dessert, but can also be served, as can the classic cakes, as a special treat with coffee on any occasion when you are entertaining.

Gâteaux do take some time to prepare, but the result is always worthwhile. The main advantage is that most gâteaux have to be assembled and even completed well in advance, thus cutting down on the time needed for last-minute preparations. Although the gâteaux do involve more time-consuming decorating, the classic cakes in this chapter use simple and quick decoration ideas for those who want to bake and decorate a cake quickly. These cakes rely on the icing (frosting) and natural ingredients, such as fruit and nuts, for finishing touches. Always choose the best quality and most perfectly shaped ingredients you can find if you are using them for decorating purposes, and use them lavishly; it really does make a difference to the final effect.

Malakoff Gâteau (page 46)

Chocolate Flower Gâteau

A luscious-looking cake that needs a bit of patience to work with the ornate chocolate decoration. The chocolate cones can be made in advance and stored in an airtight container until you need them.

Information	*Equipment*
No. of Servings: 8–10	20 cm/8 inch deep cake tin (pan)
Level of Difficulty: ★ ★	wire rack
	round cake board
	wallpaper scraper

Step 4

Step 5

INGREDIENTS

3 eggs

140 g/4½ oz/½ heaped cup caster (superfine) sugar

60 g/2 oz/½ cup plain (all-purpose) flour

30 g/1 oz/¼ cup cocoa powder

1 quantity Chocolate Ganache (see pages 26–27)

250 g/8 oz/8 squares chocolate, melted (see page 31)

icing (confectioners') sugar, for dredging

CHOCOLATE CONES

The chocolate needs to be the correct temperature, otherwise it will crack or it will not form curls.

Step 6

Step 7

1 Grease a 20 cm/8 inch deep round cake tin (pan) and line with baking parchment. Place the eggs and sugar in a heatproof bowl over a saucepan of boiling water and whisk until thick and pale. Sift together the flour and cocoa powder and fold into the mixture.

2 Turn the cake mixture into the tin (pan) and bake in a preheated oven at 190°C/375°F/ Gas Mark 5 for 30 minutes. Invert on a wire rack to cool.

3 Cut the cake in half horizontally and sandwich together with one third of the chocolate ganache and spread more ganache over the top and sides of the cake.

4 Cut a band of baking parchment slightly longer than the circumference of the cake and a little deeper. Spread thickly with melted chocolate and leave until set, but not brittle. Trim to the exact size of the cake.

5 Lift the baking parchment and attach the chocolate to the side of the cake, easing it gently round to cover the ganache, then peel off the paper.

6 Spread more melted chocolate on to a marble slab or other cold surface, using a palette knife (spatula), and leave to set. When it is just set, use a clean wallpaper scraper to scrape it into cones.

7 Arrange the chocolate cones on the top of the cake, starting from the outside and working towards the centre, placing the cones in overlapping layers to resemble a flower. Dredge with icing (confectioners') sugar.

Frosted Flower Gâteau

This liqueur-soaked sponge is covered with a fresh orange-flavoured butter cream and decorated with seasonal flowers. If you don't have a ring mould, use a 20 cm/8 inch round sandwich tin (layer cake pan).

Information	Equipment
No. of Servings: 10–12	23 cm/9 inch ring mould
Level of Difficulty: ★	wire rack
	round cake board
	small paintbrush
	piping bag
	star nozzle (tip)

Step 3

Step 4

INGREDIENTS

3-egg orange-flavoured
Victoria Sandwich (Sponge
Layer Cake) mixture (see
pages 12 and 13)

4 tbsp orange juice

4 tbsp orange-flavoured
liqueur

1 quantity Butter Cream (see
page 18–19), flavoured
with grated rind of 1 orange

Frosted Flowers

1 egg white

fresh flowers and leaves

fresh mint leaves

caster (superfine) sugar, for
dredging

Step 5

Step 6

1 Grease and flour a 23 cm/9 inch ring mould. Spoon the cake mixture into the mould and bake in a preheated oven at 190°C/350°F/Gas Mark 5 for 35–40 minutes until the cake springs back when pressed. Invert on to a wire rack to cool.

2 Cut the cake in half horizontally. Mix the orange juice and liqueur together and drizzle over both halves of the cake.

3 Sandwich the cake together with a quarter of the butter cream and place on a cake board. Cover the cake with the remaining butter cream and swirl with a palette knife (spatula).

4 To frost the flowers, whisk the egg white lightly with a few drops of water and, using a paintbrush, coat the flowers and leaves lightly all over with the egg white.

5 Brush off any excess, then dredge in the caster (superfine) sugar until completely coated. Place on baking parchment to dry.

6 Arrange the frosted flowers and mint leaves in clusters around the top of the cake. Pipe the remaining icing (frosting) round the bottom of the cake.

FROSTED FRUITS AND FLOWERS

If the flowers are completely coated with the egg white and sugar, they will dry out and may be kept for several weeks in the refrigerator. Fruits, such as grapes, currants and strawberries, may also be frosted in this way, but will only keep for 2 days.

Chocolate Caraque Gâteau

Scrolls of dark and white chocolate make this a really
sophisticated-looking cake. Don't worry if you don't manage long
scrolls at your first attempt – even short curls look very effective.

Information	*Equipment*
No. of servings: 10–12	20–30 cm/8–12 inch Swiss (jelly) roll tin (pan)
Level of Difficulty: ★ ★	wire rack
	rectangular cake board
	piping bag
	star nozzle (tip)

Step 4

Step 6

INGREDIENTS

2 eggs

90 g/3 oz/⅓ cup caster (superfine) sugar

grated rind of 1 orange

60 g/2 oz/½ cup plain (all-purpose) flour

1 quantity Chocolate Butter Icing (Frosting) (see pages 18–19)

125 g/4 oz/4 squares dark chocolate, melted (see page 31)

125 g/4 oz/4 squares white chocolate, melted (see page 31)

cocoa powder, for dredging

HINT

Make the scrolls with chocolate-flavoured cake covering; it sets more quickly and is more pliable.

Step 7

Step 8

1 Grease a 20–30 cm/8–12 inch Swiss (jelly) roll tin (pan) and line with baking parchment. Place the eggs, sugar and orange rind in a heatproof bowl over a saucepan of boiling water and whisk until thick and pale. Sift the flour and fold into the mixture.

2 Spoon the cake mixture into the tin (pan) and bake in a preheated oven at 190°C/375°F/Gas Mark 5 for 20–25 minutes. Invert on a wire rack and leave to cool.

3 Cut the cake into 3 equal layers and sandwich together with one-third of the chocolate butter icing (frosting).

4 Spread more icing (frosting) over the top and sides of the cake and smooth it evenly. Place the cake on a cake board.

5 To make the caraque, spread a thin layer of the melted dark chocolate on to a marble slab or cold work surface (counter), using a palette knife (spatula) to smooth it out, and leave to set. Do the same with the white chocolate.

6 Hold a long thin-bladed knife at an angle of 45° and push it across the chocolate to form long scrolls. Repeat with the white chocolate.

7 Lift the caraque on to a palette knife (spatula) and lay on top of the cake to cover it completely. Dredge with cocoa powder.

8 Pipe the remaining icing along the bottom edges of the cake.

Malakoff Gâteau

A gâteau comprising boudoir biscuits (lady-fingers) soaked in milk
that has been flavoured with brandy and coffee. It is layered with a
praline butter cream and covered in whipped cream.

Information	Equipment
No. of Servings: 8	900 g/2 lb loaf tin (pan)
Level of Difficulty: ★ ★	rolling pin
	kitchen weights
	piping bag
	large star nozzle (tip)

Step 1

INGREDIENTS

90 g/3 oz/¾ cup blanched almonds, roughly chopped

250 g/8 oz/1 cup caster (superfine) sugar

175 g/6 oz/¾ cup butter

2 egg yolks

150 ml/¼ pint/⅔ cup milk

4 tbsp brandy or rum

2 tbsp coffee flavouring (extract) or extremely strong black coffee

about 40 boudoir biscuits or sponge fingers (lady-fingers)

300 ml/½ pint/1¼ cups double (heavy) cream

1 tbsp milk

To Decorate

sliced strawberries

1 kiwi fruit, sliced

Step 4

Step 3

Step 5

1 Gently heat the almonds and half the sugar in a saucepan until they turn a caramel colour, shaking the pan frequently. Do not over-brown. Pour quickly on to some baking parchment and leave to set in a solid block.

2 Line a 900 g/2 lb loaf tin (pan) with non-stick baking parchment. Crush the almond caramel until powdery with a rolling pin.

3 Beat the butter until soft, then add the remaining sugar, and cream until light and fluffy. Beat in the egg yolks, followed by the crushed almonds. Set the nut mixture aside.

4 Combine the milk, alcohol and coffee flavouring (extract). Arrange a layer of boudoir biscuits (lady-fingers) in the base of the lined tin (pan), sugared-side downwards, and sprinkle with 3 tablespoons of the milk mixture.

5 Spread with one third of the nut mixture, cover with another layer of biscuits (lady-fingers) and sprinkle with milk. Layer the rest of the nut mixture and biscuits

(lady-fingers) soaked in milk to make a total of 3 nut layers and 4 biscuit layers. Press down evenly, cover with baking parchment and weight lightly. Chill for at least 12 hours.

6 Invert the gâteau on to a plate and peel off the paper. Whip the cream and milk together until just stiff. Use most of it to cover the gâteau; put the remainder into a piping bag fitted with a large star nozzle (tip) and pipe diagonal lines across the top. Mark wavy lines around the sides and add piped cream to the corners and sides. Decorate with sliced strawberries and kiwi fruit.

Black Forest Gâteau

This chocolate cake, flavoured with kirsch and sandwiched with cream and black cherries, has chocolate-coated sides and a cherry and chocolate top decoration.

Information	*Equipment*
No. of Servings: 10–12 Level of Difficulty: ✷ ✷	23 cm/9 inch round cake tin (pan) wire rack round cake board piping bag star nozzle (tip)

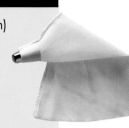

Step 4

Step 5

INGREDIENTS

3 eggs

140 g/4½ oz/½ cup plus 1 tbsp caster (superfine) sugar

90 g/3 oz/¾ cup plain (all-purpose) flour

20 g/¾ oz/3 tbsp cocoa powder

450 ml/¾ pint /2 cups double (heavy) cream

90 g/3 oz/3 squares dark chocolate

3–4 tbsp kirsch, brandy or other liqueur

1 quantity Chocolate Butter Cream (see pages 18–19)

Filling

425 g/14 oz can of stoned (pitted) black cherries, drained and juice reserved

2 tsp arrowroot

Step 6

Step 7

1 Grease a deep 23 cm/9 inch cake tin (pan) and line with non-stick baking parchment. Whisk the eggs and sugar until the mixture is very thick and pale and the whisk leaves a heavy trail when lifted.

2 Sift the flour and cocoa powder together twice, then fold evenly and lightly through the egg mixture. Pour into the prepared tin (pan) and bake in a preheated oven at 190°C/375°F/Gas Mark 5 for about 30 minutes, or until well risen and firm to the touch. Invert on a wire rack and cool.

3 To make the filling, mix 150 ml/¼ pint/⅔ cup of the juice with the arrowroot. Bring slowly to the boil, stirring continuously, and boil until clear and thickened. Reserve 8 cherries for decoration. Halve the rest and add to the sauce, then cool.

4 Whip the cream until thick enough to pipe and put 4 tablespoons into a piping bag with a large star nozzle (tip). Pare the chocolate into curls.

5 Split the cake horizontally into 3 layers. Spread the first layer with some of the cream and half the cherry mixture.

6 Cover with the second cake layer, sprinkle with the liqueur, then spread with some of the butter cream and the remaining cherry mixture. Top with the final layer of cake. Cover the sides with the rest of the butter cream.

7 Spread the remaining whipped cream over the top of the gâteau and press the chocolate curls around the sides. Pipe 8 whirls of cream on the top. Add a reserved cherry to each whirl. Chill for 2–3 hours.

Sherry & Spice Cake

The sutlanas (golden raisins) are simmered in sherry before they are baked in a layered cake which is sandwiched together with a sherry-flavoured butter cream.

Information	Equipment
No. of Servings: 8–10	2 × 20 cm/8 inch sandwich tins (layer pans)
Level of Difficulty: ✫	wire rack
	round cake board
	piping bag
	large star nozzle (tip)

Step 1

Step 2

INGREDIENTS

6 tbsp sherry

175 g/6 oz/1 cup sultanas (golden raisins)

125 g/4 oz/½ cup butter or margarine

125 g/4 oz/⅔ cup light soft brown sugar

2 eggs

175 g/6 oz/1½ cups plain (all-purpose) flour

1 tsp bicarbonate of soda (baking soda)

½ tsp ground cloves

¼ tsp ground or grated nutmeg

½ tsp ground cinnamon

60 g/2 oz/½ cup walnuts, chopped

To Decorate

1 egg yolk

1 tbsp sherry

1 quantity Butter Cream (see pages 18–19)

icing (confectioners') sugar, for dredging

walnut or pecan halves

Step 3

Step 5

1 Grease 2 × 20 cm/8 inch sandwich tins (layer pans) and line the bases with non-stick baking parchment. Bring the sherry, sultanas (golden raisins) and 4 tablespoons water to the boil. Cover and simmer for 15 minutes. Strain off the liquid, reserving the fruit, and make it up to 5 tablespoons with cold water.

2 Cream the butter and sugar until pale and fluffy. Beat in the eggs one at a time, following each with a spoonful of flour. Sift the remaining flour with the bicarbonate of soda (baking soda) and spices, and fold into the mixture with the cooled sultana (golden raisin) liquor.

3 Add the nuts and reserved sultanas (golden raisins), and mix lightly. Divide between the sandwich tins (layer pans). Level the tops.

4 Bake in a preheated oven at 180°C/350°F/Gas Mark 4 for 25–35 minutes, until firm to the touch. Cool briefly in the tins (pans), loosen the edges and invert the cakes on to a wire rack to cool.

5 To make the icing (frosting), beat the egg yolk and sherry into the butter cream. Add a little sifted icing (confectioners') sugar to thicken, if necessary. Use half the butter cream to sandwich the cakes together, then sift icing (confectioners') sugar lightly over the top of the cake.

6 Place the remaining butter cream in a piping bag fitted with a large star nozzle (tip) and pipe a row of elongated shells (see page 33) around the top, about 2.5 cm/1 inch in from the edge. Complete the decoration with pecan or walnut halves.

Carrot Cake

This delicious moist cake, full of carrots, apples, pecan nuts and spice with a soft cheese topping, was originally an American favourite, but is now popular in many other countries. The sweet topping is balanced by the wholesome ingredients in the cake, and it is great served with coffee as a mid-afternoon treat. The cake can either be left plain or dredged with icing (confectioners') sugar.

Information	Equipment
No. of Servings: 8–10	20 cm/8 inch round cake tin (pan)
Level of Difficulty: ✶	wire rack

Step 3

1 Grease a 20 cm/8 inch round cake tin (pan) and line with non-stick baking parchment.

2 Sift the flour, baking powder and cinnamon into a bowl. Mix in the brown sugar until evenly blended.

3 Grate the carrots and apples by hand or in a food processor.

4 Add the grated carrot and apple, along with the chopped nuts, to the flour mixture. Mix together lightly, then make a well in the centre.

5 Add the eggs and oil, and beat well until thoroughly blended.

Step 5

INGREDIENTS

250 g/8 oz/2 cups self-raising flour

2 tsp baking powder

1 tsp ground cinnamon

150 g/5 oz/generous ¾ cup light soft brown sugar

125 g/4 oz carrots

2 dessert (eating) apples, peeled and cored

60 g/2 oz/½ cup pecan nuts, chopped

2 eggs

150 ml/¼ pint/⅔ cup vegetable or corn oil

Topping

90 g/3 oz/⅓ cup full-fat soft cheese

90 g/3 oz/⅓ cup softened butter or margarine

175 g/6 oz/1⅓ cups icing (confectioners') sugar, sifted

grated rind of ½–1 orange

To Decorate

pecan halves

orange jelly slices

6 Spoon into the tin (pan) and level the top. Bake in a preheated oven at 180°C/350°F/Gas Mark 4 for about 1 hour, or until the cake is golden brown and just slightly shrinking from the sides of the tin (pan). Test by inserting a skewer in the centre of the cake; it should come out clean. Invert on to a wire rack and leave until cold.

Step 6

7 To make the topping, put all the ingredients together in a bowl and beat well until smooth. Spread over the top of the cake and swirl with a round-bladed knife or palette knife (spatula). As it sets, decorate with pecan halves and orange jelly slices.

Step 7

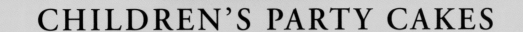

CHILDREN'S PARTY CAKES

Novelty cakes for children can be the most rewarding cakes to decorate. Although they will take considerable time to make and perfect, you will be able to really use your imagination and indulge in brighter, more vivid, colours and designs than you would use for more sophisticated cakes. You can use the recipes on the following pages as they are given, or adapt the designs and colours to suit your individual preferences. You may like to personalize the cakes by adding the child's name.

Always allow plenty of time to make the cake and leave it to rest for at least 12 hours, then to prepare and colour the icing, as well as to actually cut and assemble the cake. You must also allow time for the cake to set after the decoration has been completed, so it is best to arrange for it to be finished two or three days before the party. With cakes decorated with moulded animals or other shapes it is best to make these several days in advance if possible, to give them sufficient time to dry; otherwise, they may mark the cake; be particularly careful with the pandas (see page 67), which are made with black sugarpaste. The shapes can be made several weeks in advance and will keep almost indefinitely once dried.

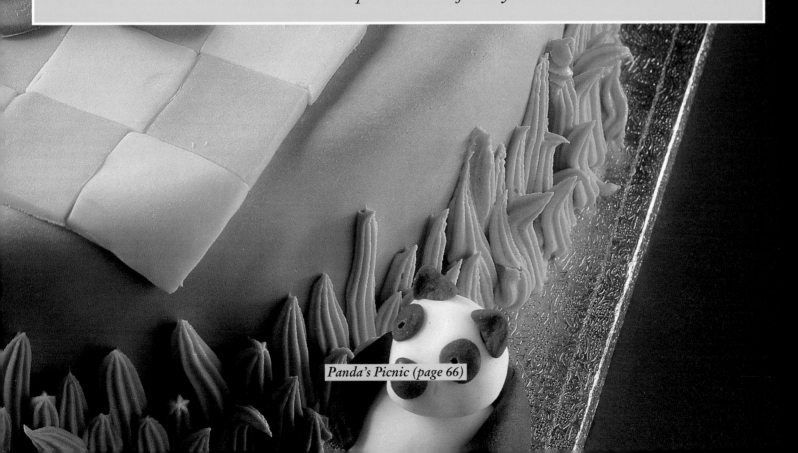

Panda's Picnic (page 66)

Happy Lion

This smiling-faced lion made from sponge cake with a butter cream and marzipan decoration will delight children and parents alike. It is perfect for a jungle themed party.

Information	Equipment
No. of servings: 10–12	23 cm/9 inch round deep cake tin (pan)
Level of Difficulty: ✭ ✭	wire rack
Advance Preparation: 1 day	round cake board
	piping bag
	large star nozzle (tip)

Step 2

Step 4

Step 5

Step 6

1 Grease and line a 23 cm/9 inch deep round cake tin (pan). Spoon in the cake mixture. Bake in a preheated oven at 160°C/325°F/ Gas Mark 3, allowing about 50–60 minutes (1–1¼ hours for Quick Mix and Madeira (Pound) Cake). Invert on a wire rack and leave for 12–24 hours.

2 Place on a cake board. Using a sharp serrated knife, pare off a piece from the top edge of the cake and place it around the base, attaching with jam; then brush the whole cake with jam.

3 Cover the top of the cake with 250 g/8 oz/2 cups yellow sugarpaste or marzipan. Reserve the remaining trimmings.

4 Put the butter cream into a piping bag fitted with a large star nozzle (tip) and pipe a circle of elongated stars, beginning about 2.5 cm/1 inch up the side of the cake and taking them out towards the edge of the cake board. Then

pipe 2 more circles, the third row beginning about 2.5 cm/1 inch in from the top edge on the lion's face, taking it part way down the side of the cake.

5 Roll out half the remaining marzipan or sugarpaste and cut out 2 circles of about 5 cm/2 inches for the ears. Colour a scrap of the

INGREDIENTS

4-egg Victoria Sandwich (Sponge Layer Cake), Quick Mix Cake or Madeira (Pound) Cake mixture (see pages 11–13)

4 tbsp apricot jam, sieved (strained)

350 g/12 oz/3 cups Marzipan or Sugarpaste (see pages 21 or 29), coloured yellow

yellow, brown and red liquid or paste food colourings

3 quantities Coffee Butter Cream (see page 19)

2 chocolate buttons or beans

few pieces of thin spaghetti

trimmings red for a mouth. Colour the remainder deep brown, roll it out and cut out 2 × 2.5 cm/1 inch circles. Place one in each ear circle. Cut out 2 × 4 cm/1½ inch rounds for eyes and mould the rest into a pointed nose. From the reserved yellow trimmings, form 2 wedges for the muzzle.

6 Squeeze the base of the ears together and attach to the cake with butter cream. Position the eyes, the mouth, the nose and muzzle and attach with butter cream. Use chocolate buttons for eyes and add a small dot of butter cream to each. Stick pieces of spaghetti into the muzzle for whiskers. Leave to set.

Baba the Lamb

Butter cream and sugarpaste are used to create this black-faced
woolly lamb in a meadow of flowers.

Information	Equipment
No. of Servings: 18	30 × 25 cm/12 × 10 inch roasting tin (pan)
Level of Difficulty: ★ ★	wire rack
Advance Preparation: 1 day	rectangular cake board
	stiff paper or card (board)
	piping bag
	small star nozzles (tips)

Step 2

INGREDIENTS

6-egg Victoria Sandwich (Sponge Layer Cake) or Madeira (Pound) Cake mixture (see pages 12–13)

6 tbsp apricot jam, sieved (strained)

350 g/12 oz/3 cups Sugarpaste (see pages 20–21)

black, green, blue, yellow and pink liquid or paste food colourings

3 quantities Butter Cream (see pages 18–19), flavoured with vanilla flavouring (extract)

few sugar mimosa balls

Step 4

Step 3

Step 5

1 Grease and line a 30 × 25 cm/ 12 × 10 inch roasting tin (pan). Spread the cake mixture evenly in it. Bake in a preheated oven at 160°C/325°F/Gas Mark 3 for about 50–60 minutes (1–1¼ hours for Madeira (Pound) Cake) or until firm to the touch. Invert on a wire rack and leave for 12–24 hours.

2 Trim the cake and place upside-down on a cake board. Draw the shape of a lamb on a piece of stiff paper or card (board), cut out and position on the cake. The ears and tail can be cut from the cake trimmings. Cut round the template. Cut out and attach the ears and tail with jam. Then brush the cake all over with jam.

3 Colour 90 g/3 oz/¾ cup of the sugarpaste green and roll out thinly. Use to cover the board around the lamb's legs and body up to sky level, attaching it with jam. Color 60 g/2 oz/½ cup sugarpaste blue for the sky, roll it out thinly and use to cover the rest of the cake board.

4 Colour the remaining sugarpaste black or brownish-black and roll out thinly. Use to cover the head and ears of the lamb, and then the legs, pressing evenly to the cake. Trim off where it meets the grass and sky.

5 Add a touch of yellow food colouring to three-quarters of the butter cream. Put it into a piping bag fitted with a small star nozzle (tip) and pipe stars all over the body and tail to touch the head, legs, sky and grass. Add a small star for each eye with a dot of black sugarpaste in the centres. Add a black sugarpaste nose.

6 Colour a tablespoon of the remaining butter cream pink, and the remainder grass green. Put both into piping bags fitted with star nozzles (tips). Pipe rough patches of grass on the cake board, as in the photograph. Add stars of pink butter cream for daisies and complete with mimosa balls.

Racing Car

Racing cars come in all shapes and sizes, are usually brightly coloured and can be traditional or modern. Shape the cake to the design of the car you like best.

Information	Equipment
No. of Servings: 14–16	28 × 18 × 4 cm/11 × 7 × 1½ inches roasting tins (pans)
Level of Difficulty: ★ ★ ★	wire racks
Advance Preparation: 1 day	rectangular cake board
	piping bag
	writing nozzle (tip)
	cocktail sticks (toothpicks)

Step 3

1 Grease 2 roasting tins (pans) measuring 28 × 18 × 4 cm/ 11 × 7 × 1½ inches, and line with baking parchment. Spread the cake mixture evenly in the tins (pans). Bake in a preheated oven at 160°C/ 325°F/Gas Mark 3 for about 45–50 minutes until firm. Invert on wire racks and let set for 12–24 hours.

2 Trim the cakes to a width of 11 cm/4½ inches wide, reserving the trimmings. Sandwich the cakes together with jam. Slightly taper one end of the cake and round the other end for the back of the car. About 10 cm/4 inches from the back of the car cut out a wedge through the top layer of cake for the seat. Use a piece of the cake

Step 4

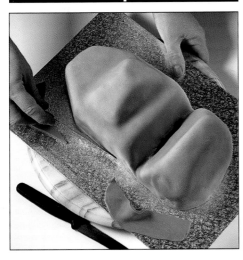

trimmings to build up the car behind the seat. Add a small elongated triangular piece of cake to the top of the bonnet (hood), attaching all with jam.

3 From the other trimmings, cut out 2 wheels of 5 cm/2 inches and 2 of 6 cm/2½ inches. The larger back wheels should be wider than the front ones. Brush the car and tires with jam.

4 Colour 625 g/1¼ lb/5 cups of the sugarpaste bright blue. Roll out and use to cover the entire car, moulding to fit all the undulations, but cutting out a piece for the seat so it does not split.

5 Colour 250 g/8 oz/2 cups of the sugarpaste black. Roll out and use a piece to fit inside the seat area

Step 5

of the car, and to cover the tyres. Mark treads on the tyres with a sharp knife, then attach with cocktail sticks (toothpicks) and a dab of royal icing. Also mould a steering wheel, an anti-roll bar to put behind the seat, and 2 wing mirrors, and attach.

6 Colour the remaining sugarpaste grey, and use for a seat in the car, a front radiator, and trims to the wheels. Colour the royal icing grey and using a No. 2 writing nozzle (tip), pipe spokes on the tyres and a radiator grille on the car. Pipe the age of the child for the car number and, if liked, a name or message on the car or board. Leave to set.

Step 6

My Pony

An ideal cake for a child who is mad about horses. Simply find out the colour of his or her favourite pony and make the icing (frosting) the same colour.

Information	Equipment
No. of Servings: 18	30 × 25 cm/12 × 10 inch roasting tin (pan)
Level of Difficulty: ★	wire rack
Advance Preparation: 1 day	rectangular cake board
	stiff paper or card (board)
	cocktail stick (toothpick)
	piping bag
	star nozzle (tip)

Step 5

Step 6

Step 7

Step 8

1 Grease and line a roasting tin (pan), 30 × 25 cm/12 × 10 inches. Spread the cake mixture evenly in it. Bake in a preheated oven at 160°C/325°F/Gas Mark 3 for about 50–60 minutes (1–1¼ hours for Quick Mix Cake). Invert on a wire rack and leave for 24 hours.

2 Trim the cake, place upside-down on a cake board and brush all over with the apricot jam. Colour 250 g/8 oz/2 cups of the sugarpaste sky blue, roll out and lay over the top third of the cake, giving it a slightly uneven edge. Trim off around the base neatly.

3 Colour about 425 g/14 oz/3½ cups of the sugarpaste grass green. Roll out and use to cover the rest of the cake, matching it evenly to the sky, and trim off neatly around the base.

4 Draw a picture of a horse on stiff paper or card (board) and cut out to make a template.

5 Colour about 175 g/6 oz/1½ cups of the sugarpaste the colour of the pony and roll it out large enough to place the template on. Cut carefully around the template. Gently remove the template and then carefully move the horse to the top of the cake, dampening in places so it will stick.

6 Roll out the trimmings and make a mane, tail and forelock, marking with a knife to make it

INGREDIENTS

6-egg chocolate-flavoured Victoria Sandwich (Sponge Layer Cake) or Quick Mix Cake mixture (see pages 11–13)

6 tbsp apricot jam, sieved (strained)

875 g/1¾ lb/7 cups Sugarpaste (see pages 20–21)

green, blue, black and brown liquid or paste food colouring

1 quantity Butter Cream (see pages 18–19)

long chocolate matchsticks

look realistic. Mark in the features with a cocktail stick (toothpick).

7 Place the chocolate matchsticks on the cake to form a fence, attaching with butter cream.

8 Colour the butter cream grass green and put into a piping bag fitted with a star nozzle (tip). Pipe squiggly lines to make a hedge at each end of the fence plus a couple of trees (adding chocolate matchsticks for trunks). Use the remaining butter cream to pipe uneven lengths of grass up the sides of the cake to attach to the board, and random patches of grass on the cake.

Hot Air Balloon

This pretty, brightly coloured hot air balloon with a basket underneath it is
decorated all over with sugarpaste or marzipan shapes.

Information	Equipment
No. of Servings: 10–12	23 cm/9 inch ovenproof bowl
Level of Difficulty: ☆ ☆	wire rack
Advance Preparation: 1 day	rectangular cake board
	small decorative cutters or a sharp knife
	piping bags
	small star nozzles (tips)

Step 3

Step 4

INGREDIENTS

4-egg Victoria Sandwich (Sponge Layer Cake), Quick Mix Cake or Madeira (Pound) Cake mixture (see pages 11–13)

6 tbsp apricot jam, sieved (strained)

1 kg/2 lb/8 cups Sugarpaste or Marzipan (see pages 21 or 29)

yellow, orange, green and mauve liquid or paste food colourings

1 quantity Butter Cream (see pages 18–19)

4 wooden skewers

Step 5

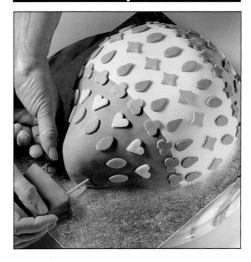

Step 6

1 Grease a 23 cm/9 inch ovenproof bowl (about 2.25 litres/4 pints/2½ quart capacity) thoroughly. Spoon the cake mixture into the bowl, making sure it is evenly distributed, and level the top. Bake in a preheated oven at 160°C/325°F/Gas Mark 3 for about 1¼–1½ hours until firm to the touch and a skewer inserted in the centre comes out clean. Invert on a wire rack and let set for 24 hours.

2 Place the cake upside-down on a rectangular cake board and brush all over with the jam. Take about 125 g/4 oz/1 cup of the sugarpaste or marzipan and mould a piece to put at the base of the balloon to make it elongated.

3 Colour about 175 g/6 oz/ 1½ cups of the sugarpaste or marzipan mauve, then divide the remainder into 3 pieces and colour them yellow, orange and green respectively. Roll out about three-quarters of each of the 3 large pieces of sugarpaste or marzipan and use each to form a wide stripe around the balloon, so it is completely covered.

4 Shape 125 g/4 oz/1 cup of the mauve sugarpaste or marzipan into a small rectangle for the basket. Cut out various shapes in the different colours of sugarpaste or marzipan with a cutter or a

sharp knife and attach them in even bands to the balloon to make it as pretty and vibrant as possible.

5 Attach the rectangular piece of sugarpaste or marzipan for the basket at the base of the balloon and stick the skewers into the basket and the base of the balloon to represent the ropes, as shown.

6 Colour half the butter cream green and the remainder orange. Put into piping bags fitted with small star nozzles (tips) and use to decorate both the basket and the balloon. Use a spare piece of green sugarpaste to make a banner and pipe on a message with the buttercream, if liked. Leave to set.

Panda's Picnic

A pretty round decorated cake shows a charming picnic scene with
moulded sugarpaste pandas.

Information	*Equipment*
No. of Servings: 10–12	23 cm/9 inch deep round cake tin (pan)
Level of Difficulty: ✭ ✭	square cake board
Advance Preparation: 1 day	cocktail sticks (toothpicks)
	red icing (frosting) pen
	piping bag
	small star nozzle (tip)

Step 3

Step 4

Step 5

Step 6

1 Grease and line a 23 cm/9 inch deep round cake tin (pan). Spread the cake mixture evenly in it. Bake in a preheated oven at 160°C/325°F/Gas Mark 3 for about 1–1¼ hours, or until firm. Invert on a wire rack and leave to set for 12–24 hours. Trim the cake and place upside-down on a 28 cm/11 inch cake board. Brush all over with the jam.

2 Colour 625 g/1¼ lb/5 cups of the sugarpaste green. Roll out, use to cover the cake and trim.

3 Colour 90 g/3 oz/⅜ cup of the sugarpaste pale yellow and another 90 g/3 oz/⅜ cup orange. Roll out and cut each colour into 18 pieces, 2.5 cm/1 inch square. Arrange on the cake to make a tablecloth, dampening to stick.

4 Colour 375 g/12 oz/3 cups of the sugarpaste black and leave 175 g/6 oz/1½ cups white for the pandas. Make 6 pandas; each needs about 90 g/3 oz/⅜ cup sugarpaste. Form balls for the heads and bodies and black U shapes for the legs. Attach the legs, bodies and heads by inserting a cocktail stick (toothpick) through each panda. Add eyes, noses and ears in black and mark features with a cocktail stick (toothpick). Leave to dry.

5 Colour about 90 g/3 oz/⅜ cup of the sugarpaste bright blue. Roll out thinly and cut out 3 plates of about 4 cm/ 1½ inches and 6 of 2 cm/¾ inch. Using a finger, press

INGREDIENTS

4-egg Madeira (Pound) Cake or Quick Mix Cake mixture (see pages 11–13)

5 tbsp apricot jam, sieved (strained)

1.5 kg/3 lb/12 cups Sugarpaste (see pages 20–21)

green, black, orange, yellow, blue and brown liquid or paste food colourings

1 quantity Butter Cream (see pages 18–19)

into the centre of the plates to give a rim. Mould 6 cups or mugs out of the trimmings. Roll out a little of the white sugarpaste and cut into sandwiches. Draw around the sides with an icing (frosting) pen and place on one of the large plates. Colour the rest of the sugarpaste brown and shape into a cake.

6 Arrange the plates and mugs on the tablecloth, dampening to attach. Colour the butter cream grass green and put into a piping bag fitted with a small star nozzle (tip). Pipe strands of butter cream part way up on the sides of the cake from the base upwards to represent grass. Arrange the pandas on top of the cake and by the side.

Hickory Dickory Dock Cake

The hands of the clock can point to the age of the child, and the colourings can be varied to suit individual preferences.

Information	Equipment
No. of Servings: 18	23 cm/9 inch square cake tin (pan)
Level of Difficulty: ✿ ✿ ✿	23 cm/9 inch deep round cake tin (pan)
Advance Preparation: 1 day	wire racks
	rectangular cake board
	cocktail sticks (toothpicks)
	artificial flower stamens
	piping bag and writing nozzle (tip)

1 Grease and line a 23 cm/9 inch square cake tin (pan) and a 23 cm/9 inch deep round cake tin (pan). Spread the 3-egg cake mixture in the square tin (pan) and the 4-egg mixture in the round tin (pan). Bake in a preheated oven at 160°C/325°F/Gas Mark 3, about 1¼–1½ hours for the round cake and 50–60 minutes for the square. Invert on wire racks and leave to set for 12–24 hours.

2 Halve the square cake vertically and sandwich together with 4 tablespoons of the jam. Place on a cake board and cut out a deep dip so the round cake fits into it. Trim the round cake evenly. Brush both cakes with jam.

3 Colour half the sugarpaste pale blue. Roll it and use it to cover the cake on the board. Cover the other cake's sides with two-thirds of the blue sugarpaste and push into the dip in the first cake.

4 Colour a third of the remaining sugarpaste dark blue and half green. Roll out some of the green sugarpaste and use to cover the face of the clock, just overlapping the edge; then crimp it attractively. Roll the blue and the rest of the green sugarpaste into long sausage shapes. Twist together and place around the base of the clock face.

5 Use a scrap of the pale blue sugarpaste to form clock hands and attach to the face. Use the remaining pieces of sugarpaste to shape into mice with 2 ears, a long tail, teardrop-shaped body and a black nose, and mark the eyes with a cocktail stick (toothpick). Insert some short lengths of flower stamens for whiskers. Leave to dry.

6 Using royal icing and a piping bag fitted with a star nozzle (tip), pipe a border of stars around the base of the bottom end of the clock. Pipe small stars on the sides of the clock face and base, and a twisted circle on the face about 2.5 cm/1 inch in from the edge. With a No. 2 writing nozzle (tip), pipe the numbers on the clock and write 'Happy Birthday' and the child's name on the base of the cake. Pipe any extra decorations you might like on the clock. Leave to set, then attach the mice on and around the clock and leave to dry.

Step 3

Step 4

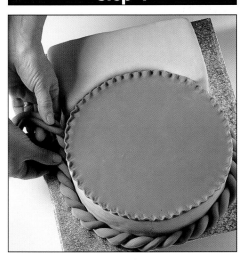

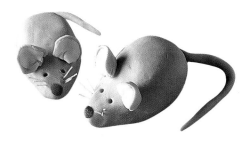

INGREDIENTS

3-egg and 4-egg Quick Mix Cake mixture (see pages 11 and 13)

10 tbsp apricot jam, sieved (strained)

1 kg/2 lb/8 cups Sugarpaste (see pages 20–21)

blue, green and black liquid or paste food colourings

250 g/8 oz/2 cups Royal Icing (see pages 20–21)

Step 5

Step 6

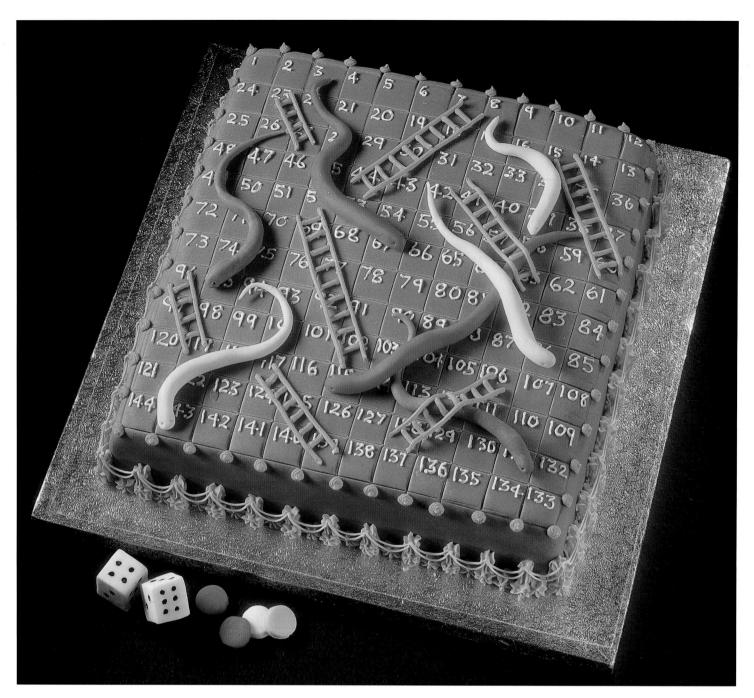

Snakes & Ladders Cake

This is a very popular game which can be played by children at a party before the cake is cut.

Information	Equipment
No. of Servings: 18	25 cm/10 inch square cake pan (tin)
Level of Difficulty: ✹ ✹	wire rack
Advance Preparation: 1 day	square cake board
	piping bag
	small and large writing nozzles (tips)
	star nozzle (tip)

Step 2

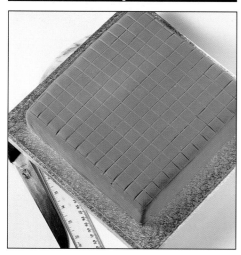

5-egg quantity Victoria Sandwich (Sponge Layer Cake) or Madeira (Pound) Cake mixture, any flavour (see pages 12–13)

5 tbsp apricot jam, sieved (strained)

1 kg/2 lb/8 cups Sugarpaste (see pages 20–21)

green, blue, yellow, red, orange and black liquid or paste food colourings

1 quantity Royal Icing (see pages 20–21)

Step 5

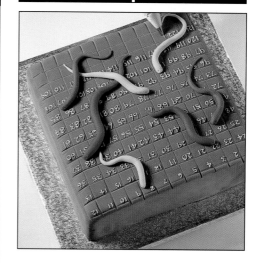

1 Grease and line a 25 cm/10 inch square cake tin (pan). Spread the cake mixture evenly in it. Bake in a preheated oven at 160°C/325°F/ Gas Mark 3 for about 1–1¼ hours or until firm to the touch. Invert on a wire rack and leave to set for 12–24 hours.

2 Trim the cake and place upside-down on a cake board. Brush all over with jam.

3 Colour about 750 g/1½ lb/6 cups of the sugarpaste green and use to cover the whole cake, trimming off evenly around the base. Using the back of a knife, mark the top of the cake into 2 cm/¾ inch squares. Leave to set.

VARIATION

The colour scheme of this cake can be changed to suit your taste. Try a basic colouring of red, blue or yellow.

5 Colour about half the royal icing pale green, put into a piping bag fitted with a writing nozzle (tip) and pipe numbers on all the squares; then, using a star nozzle (tip), pipe a decoration around the base of the cake with alternate stars and elongated stars. Add loops from star to star with the writing nozzle (tip).

6 Colour the remaining royal icing orange and put into a piping bag fitted with a large writing nozzle (tip). Pipe ladders on the cake, as in the photograph. Finally, use the remaining sugarpaste to make into square dice; add tiny dots of black food colouring to complete the dice.

Step 4

4 Colour about 60 g/2 oz/¼ cup each of the sugarpaste red, blue and yellow, and shape these into snakes of various lengths. Place them on the board, as in the photograph. Also shape 4 round counters about 1 cm/½ inch across, each one coloured in a different colour, either red, blue, yellow or white.

Step 6

Playing-Card Cake

This very simple novelty cake can be adapted to any card suit.

Information	Equipment
No. of Servings: 10–12	28 × 18/11 × 7 inch cake tin (pan)
Level of Difficulty: ✷	rectangular cake board
Advance Preparation: 1 day	serrated icing scraper
	stiff paper or card (board)
	large and small heart-shaped cutters
	piping bag and small wrting nozzle (tip)

Step 2

Step 3

INGREDIENTS

2-egg Victoria Sandwich (Sponge Layer Cake) mixture (see pages 12–13)

1 quantity blue Butter Icing (Frosting) (see pages 18–19)

250 g/8 oz/1 cup white Sugarpaste (see pages 20–21)

60 g/2 oz/½ cup red Sugarpaste (see pages 20–21)

60 g/2 oz/½ cup red Royal Icing (see pages 20–21)

egg white

TO MAKE A TEMPLATE

Draw the exact shape of the top of the cake on to a piece of baking parchment. Cut a piece of card (board) to the same size to make the template.

HINT

If you don't have heart-shaped cutters, use a sharp knife to cut the sugarpaste into diamonds.

Step 4

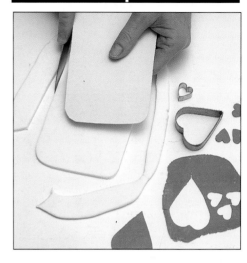

Step 5

1 Grease a shallow 28 × 18 cm/ 11 × 7 inch cake tin (pan) and line with baking parchment. Spoon the cake mixture into the tin (pan) and bake in a preheated oven at 190°C/375°F/Gas Mark 5 for 30 minutes. Cool on a wire rack.

2 Trim the cake to an oblong measuring 20 × 16 cm/8 × 6½ inches. Cut the cake in half horizontally and sandwich it together with some of the butter icing (frosting). Round off the corners slightly and place on a cake board. Discard the excess cake.

3 Cover the top and sides with butter icing (frosting), making the top as smooth as possible and using a serrated icing scraper round the sides of the cake.

4 Roll out the white sugarpaste and, using a template, cut to the exact size of the top of the cake. Lift on a rolling pin, lay on the cake and smooth evenly (see pages 22–23).

5 Roll out the red sugarpaste and use cutters to cut out 1 large heart and 4 smaller hearts. Attach to the top of the cake with egg white. Pipe the letter A over the hearts and lines as shown using red royal icing.

SPECIAL OCCASION CAKES

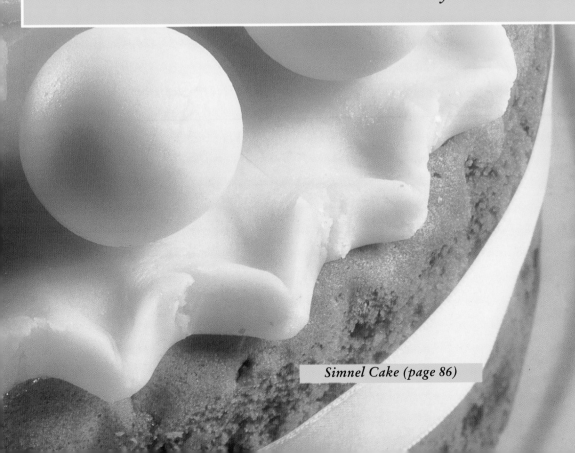

In this chapter you will find a wide range of cakes for all those special occasions throughout the year. Along with cakes for Valentine's Day, Mother's Day, Easter and Christmas, there are birthday, anniversary, christening and wedding cakes. For Easter, there is a traditional Simnel Cake, with a layer of marzipan baked in the centre, a marzipan topping and eleven marzipan balls, said to represent the faithful disciples. There are some enchanting Christmas cakes, especially one decorated as a stocking and another as a sleigh.

As with the Children's Party Cakes, these cakes show how to use piping, moulding and other decorative techniques to best advantage to create dramatic effects. The cakes can be adapted as you like, adding personalized messages or names, changing the colours of the icing (frosting), or substituting some of the decorations and designs with others used in the book. Although some of the decorations are rather complicated, you may like to extract one or two of the techniques and use them on a simpler cake. When decorating, it is a good idea to stand back from the cake occasionally and take a look at how the design is developing; it is very easy to over-pipe or over-decorate, and a design can become chaotic and untidy as a result.

Simnel Cake (page 86)

Christmas Rose Cake

Delicate Christmas roses make an elegant Christmas decoration. If you prefer a more simple finish, you could cut out a small Christmas tree shape and use this in place of the flowers.

Information	*Equipment*
No. of Servings: 20	square cake board
Level of Difficulty: ★	piping bag
Advance Preparation: 1 day	star nozzle (tip)
	cocktail stick (toothpick)
	No. 1 and No. 2 writing nozzles (tips)

Step 3

1 Cover the cake with 3 layers of royal icing (see pages 24–25). Allow the icing to dry between each coat.

2 Ice the cake board (see page 85).

3 Fit a piping bag with a No. 43 star nozzle (tip) and half-fill with royal icing. Pipe a row of shells around the top and bottom edges of the cake (see page 33).

Step 4

INGREDIENTS

20 cm/8 inch square Rich Fruit Cake (see page 12), covered in Marzipan (see pages 28–29)

2 quantities Royal Icing (see pages 20–21)

½ quantity Sugarpaste (see pages 20–21)

red and yellow food colouring

HINTS

Make the Christmas roses well in advance and store in an airtight container in the refrigerator until required.

Instead of piping stamens in the Christmas roses, you can insert bought flower stamens into the holes made with a cocktail stick (toothpick).

4 Using the same nozzle (tip), pipe another row of shells at each corner.

5 Shape a piece of sugarpaste the size of a pea into a petal, as for the rose on page 37. Make 4 more petals, pinch on to a small cone of icing. Leave to dry.

Step 5

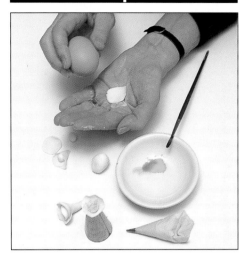

6 Mark the centre of the flower with a cocktail stick (toothpick), then paint the centre of the flower with yellow food colouring.

7 Using yellow royal icing and a No. 1 writing nozzle (tip), pipe stamens into the centre and leave to dry. Make 2 more roses.

8 Using red royal icing and a No. 2 writing nozzle (tip), pipe lines on the sides and on top of the cake, as shown. Pipe 'Merry Christmas', 'Festive Greetings' or your own personal message as you prefer, and arrange the roses on top of the cake.

Step 8

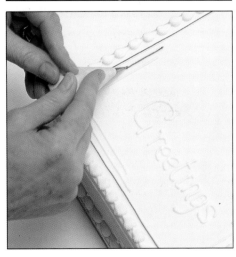

Christmas Stocking

This cake idea makes a festive gift for a friend or can be served at a Christmas party or for a family treat.

Information	Equipment
No. of Servings: 18	30 × 25 cm/12 × 10 inch roasting tin (pan)
Level of Difficulty: ✵ ✵	wire rack
Advance Preparation: 1 day	stiff paper or card (board)
	rectangular cake board
	holly leaf cutter
	piping bag
	star and writing nozzles (tips)

1 Grease and line a 30 × 25 cm/ 12 × 10 inch roasting tin (pan). Spread the cake mixture evenly in it. Bake in a preheated oven at 160°C/325°F/Gas Mark 3 for 50–60 minutes (1–1¼ hours for Quick Mix and Madeira (Pound) Cake) until well risen and firm to the touch. Invert on a wire rack and leave to set for 12–24 hours.

2 Draw a stocking shape on stiff paper or card (board) the same size as the cake and draw 3 or 4 shapes to use for parcels. Cut out, place on the cake and cut around the templates. Place the stocking on a cake board and brush all over with jam. Brush all over the pieces of cake for the parcels too.

3 Colour three-quarters of the sugarpaste red. Roll out and use to cover the stocking (see pages 22–23). Trim off around the base. Make about 6 holly berries by rolling small balls of the paste.

4 Colour 90 g/3 oz/¾ cup of the sugarpaste green. Roll it out and cut out 18 holly leaves with cutters. Use the remaining green paste to cover one of the parcels.

5 Colour half the remaining sugarpaste blue and the rest yellow. Roll out the yellow sugarpaste and cut 2 strips about 2 cm/¾ inch wide and some small stars. Place the strips across the stocking. Use the remainder to

cover another of the parcels. Do the same with the blue sugarpaste. Place the stars and holly leaves in position on the strips.

6 Put some of the royal icing into a piping bag fitted with a star nozzle (tip) and the rest into a bag with a writing nozzle (tip). Use the star nozzle (tip) to pipe a decorative cuff around the top of the stocking. Use the writing nozzle (tip) to write 'Happy Christmas' and attach the holly leaves and berries in bunches. Tie ribbons around the parcels and position at the top of the stocking together with the chocolate coins. Leave to set.

Step 2

Step 4

INGREDIENTS

6-egg quantity Victoria Sandwich (Sponge Layer Cake), Quick Mix Cake or Madeira (Pound) Cake mixture, any flavour (see pages 11–13)

6 tbsp apricot jam, sieved (strained)

750 g/1½ lb/6 cups Sugarpaste (see pages 20–21)

red, green, yellow and blue liquid or paste food colourings

500 g/1 lb/4 cups Royal Icing (see pages 20–21)

narrow Christmas ribbons

chocolate coins

Step 5

Step 6

Santa's Sleigh

A pretty cake with piles of Christmas presents ready for Santa to
deliver to the children makes a wonderful centrepiece or feature on
a table before it is served.

Information	Equipment
No. of Servings: 10–12	23 cm/9 inch square cake tin (pan)
Level of Difficulty: ★ ★ ★	wire rack
Advance Preparation: 1 day	rectangular cake board
	piping bag
	star nozzle (tip)

Step 2

Step 3

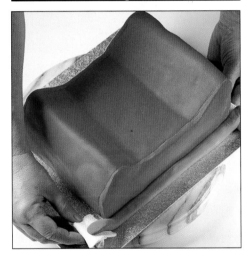

1 Grease and line a 23 cm/9 inch square cake tin (pan). Spread the cake mixture evenly in it. Bake in a preheated oven at 160°C/325°F/Gas Mark 3 for about 1–1¼ hours (1¼–1½ hours for Madeira (Pound) Cake) until well risen and firm. Turn out and leave on a wire rack for 12–24 hours to set.

2 Trim the cake and cut a 13 cm/6 inch slice off one side. Cut the slice to the same width as the sleigh, then cut in half diagonally

and place one piece on each end, as in the photograph. Place the cake on a board. Trim the remaining piece to make a sack.

3 Brush the cake all over with jam. Colour about 500 g/1 lb/4 cups of the sugarpaste red. Roll out and use to cover the cake (see pages 22–23). Colour 175 g/6 oz/1½ cups of the sugarpaste brown; use 90 g/3 oz/¾ cup to make 2 rolls about 28 cm/11 inches long and place along the base of the sleigh each side for runners. Tilt each end up slightly and put paper towels underneath to hold them in place.

4 Colour the butter cream deep cream and place in a piping bag fitted with a star nozzle (tip). Pipe decorations around the sides of the sleigh. Use the sweets (candies) to decorate the sleigh and attach a

INGREDIENTS

5-egg Victoria Sandwich (Sponge Layer Cake) or Madeira (Pound) Cake mixture, any flavour (see pages 12–13)

6 tbsp apricot jam, sieved (strained)

875 g/1¾ lb/7 cups Sugarpaste (see pages 20–21)

red, brown, green, yellow and blue liquid or paste food colourings

1 quantity Butter Cream (see pages 18–19)

few coloured sweets (candies)

2 long chocolate matchsticks

chocolate coins and candy stick or rings (optional)

Step 4

Step 6

chocolate matchstick on each side with butter cream for the shafts.

5 Roll out the remaining brown sugarpaste and use to cover the other piece of cake for a sack; place in the sleigh. Colour the remaining sugarpaste blue, yellow and green. Form the green and blue into small parcels and wrap coloured strips round them to resemble ribbons; leave to dry. Mould tiny teddy bears from the yellow paste, mark features with a cocktail stick (toothpick), and leave to dry.

6 Arrange the parcels, chocolate coins, teddies and candy stick or rings in the sleigh, and attach with butter cream. Leave to set.

Valentine's Day Cake

If you think that the frills will be too difficult to make, fix a pink ribbon around the cake, attaching it at the top of the heart with a little royal icing.

Information	Equipment
No. of Servings: 8–10	heart-shaped cake board
Level of Difficulty: ★★	cocktail stick (toothpick)
Advance Preparation: 1 day	Garrett frill cutter or sharp knife and pin
	piping bag
	writing nozzle (tip)
	small paintbrush

Step 3

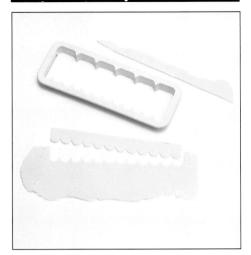

1 Cut the cake in half horizontally and sandwich together with butter icing (frosting). Brush the cake all over with apricot glaze.

2 Roll out the sugarpaste and cut out a 30 cm/12 inch heart shape. Lift the sugarpaste over the cake with a rolling pin and mould to fit (see pages 22–23). Trim off the surplus sugarpaste, roll into a ball and colour half of it pink. Leave the cake overnight to dry. Cover the cake board (see page 85).

3 Roll out the pink sugarpaste thinly and cut an oblong shape using a Garrett frill cutter or a sharp knife. If using a knife, mark out the frill with a pin before cutting, to get an even shape.

4 Place a cocktail stick (toothpick) over the edge of each flute, and roll back and forth to stretch the sugarpaste. Repeat all along to make a frill.

Step 4

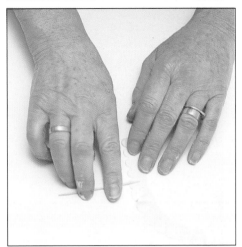

5 Moisten the straight edge of the frill and attach to the side of the cake. Make a white frill and attach above the pink. Make another pink frill and attach above the white frill.

6 Use the pink royal icing and a No. 1 writing nozzle (tip) to decorate the top of the frill, to

INGREDIENTS

3-egg Madeira (Pound) Cake, baked in an 18 cm/7 inch deep heart-shaped tin (pan) (see pages 12–13)

½ quantity Butter Icing (Frosting) (see pages 18–19)

Apricot Glaze (see pages 28–29)

1 quantity Sugarpaste (see pages 20–21)

pink food colouring

⅛ quantity pink Royal Icing (see pages 20–21)

1 egg white

rose petals

caster (superfine) sugar, for dredging

Step 5

Step 7

make a border round the top edge of the cake and to pipe names on the cake.

7 Whisk the egg white with a few drops of water and coat the rose petals lightly with a paintbrush. Dredge with caster (superfine) sugar and leave to dry before arranging on the cake.

HINT

If you knead equal quantities of flowerpaste (see page 21) and sugarpaste together, the icing (frosting) will be more malleable.

Mother's Day Cake

For an even prettier decorative effect, pipe dots on the bows using royal icing to introduce extra colour, matching it to the ribbons and roses if desired. Make the cake the day before you cover it with the butter icing (frosting) and then leave the covered cake to dry overnight before attaching the twists and bows to avoid marking the icing (frosting).

Information	Equipment
No. of Servings: 8	round cake board
Level of Difficulty: ☆	cocktail stick (toothpick)
Advance Preparation: 1–2 days	

1 Split the cake in half and sandwich with butter icing.

2 Fill in any imperfections with butter icing (frosting) and brush the cake with warm apricot glaze. Use all but 30 g/1 oz/¼ cup of the sugarpaste to cover (see pages 22–23). Leave overnight to dry.

3 Mark the cake, using a cocktail stick (toothpick), at 12 cm/ 5 inch intervals all round the side.

4 Knead the remaining 30 g/1 oz/ ¼ cup of the sugarpaste with the flowerpaste until smooth.

5 Roll half the sugarpaste into a long strip and cut 6 strips measuring 14 cm × 5 mm/ 5½ × ¼ inches.

6 Twist 1 of the strips and secure to the cake at the marks with a little egg white. Twist the remaining 5 strips and attach in the same way.

7 Roll out the remaining sugarpaste and cut 6 strips measuring 12 cm × 5 mm/5 × ¼ inches. Trim the ends as shown. Fold the ends to cross in the centre, dampen with the egg white where they all meet and press with the back of a knife to form a bow.

8 Attach the bows with egg white to the cake at the joins where 2 twists meet.

9 Arrange the roses on top of the cake and the ribbon around the base.

TO COVER THE CAKE BOARD

Moisten the cake board and cover with thinly rolled sugarpaste. Trim the sugarpaste level with the edge of the board and leave to dry before putting the cake in the centre.

Step 6

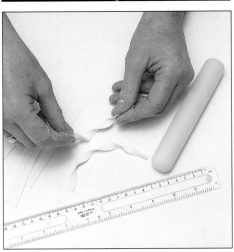

Step 7

INGREDIENTS

3-egg Madeira (Pound) Cake mixture (see pages 12–13), baked in an 18 cm/7 inch deep cake tin (pan)

½ quantity Butter Icing (Frosting) (see pages 18–19)

¾ quantity Apricot Glaze (see pages 28–29)

1 quantity Sugarpaste (see pages 20–21)

30 g/1 oz/¼ cup Flowerpaste (see page 21)

egg white

3 moulded roses (see page 37)

ribbon

Step 8

Step 9

Simnel Cake

This traditional Easter cake is a moderately rich fruit cake with a
layer of marzipan baked in the centre and a marzipan
decoration of spring daffodils on top.

Information	*Equipment*
No. of Servings: 20	18–20 cm/ 7–8 inch round cake tin (pan)
Level of Difficulty: ✷ ✷	sheets of newspaper
	wire rack
	5-petal flower cutter
	small paintbrush

Step 3

1 Line an 18–20 cm/7–8 inch cake tin (pan) with a double layer of non-stick baking parchment.

2 Sift the flour, salt and spices into a bowl. In a separate bowl, mix the dried fruits with the peel, cherries, ginger and orange rind.

3 Cream the butter and sugar together until fluffy. Beat in the eggs one at a time, following each with a spoonful of the flour. Fold in the remaining flour, followed by the fruit mixture and orange juice. Spoon half of the cake mixture evenly into the tin (pan).

4 Roll out one third of the marzipan to a circle the size of

Step 4

INGREDIENTS

250 g/8 oz/2 cups plain (all-purpose) flour

pinch of salt

1 tsp ground cinnamon

½ tsp each ground allspice and nutmeg

175 g/6 oz/1 cup sultanas (golden raisins)

125 g/4 oz/⅔ cup currants

125 g/4 oz/⅔ cup raisins

60 g/2 oz/⅓ cup cut mixed (candied) peel

60 g/2 oz/¼ cup glacé (candied) cherries, quartered, washed and dried

45 g/1½ oz/¼ cup stem ginger, chopped

grated rind of 1 orange

175 g/6 oz/¾ cup butter

175 g/6 oz/1 cup light soft brown sugar

3 eggs

1–2 tbsp orange juice

625 g/1¼ lb Marzipan (see pages 28–29)

apricot jam, sieved (strained)

orange food colouring

yellow ribbon

the tin (pan). Lay over the mixture and cover with the remaining mixture. Tie several layers of newspaper around the tin (pan).

5 Bake in a preheated oven at 160°C/ 325°F/Gas Mark 3 for 2–2½ hours until the sides are just shrinking away from the tin (pan).

Step 6

Leave 10 minutes, invert on to a wire rack and leave until cold.

6 Roll out half the marzipan into a circle and attach with jam. Decorate the edge and mark a criss-cross pattern with a knife.

7 Roll some of the remaining marzipan into 11 small balls and arrange around the edge. Roll out the remaining marzipan to make the daffodils. Cut out 8 shapes with a 5-petal flower cutter and 1.5 cm/½ inch circles. Bend the circles into cups and attach to the centre of each daffodil. Leave to dry, then paint the rims with food colouring. Arrange on the cake and finish with a ribbon.

Step 7

Twenty-first Birthday Carnation Cake

A simple design that can be adapted to suit many different occasions. Instead of the trellis work you could fill the scallop shapes with lacework (see page 33).

Information	*Equipment*
No. of Servings: 20–24	round cake board
Advance Preparation: 1 day	straight pin for marking
Level of Difficulty: ✶ ✶	piping bag
	writing nozzles (tips)
	star nozzle (tip)

Step 2

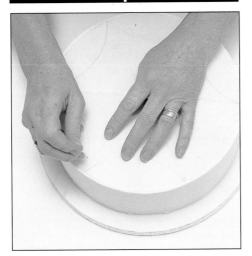

INGREDIENTS

25 cm/10 inch round Rich Fruit Cake (see pages 12 and 14), covered with Marzipan (see pages 28–29)

2 quantities white Royal Icing (see pages 20–21)

½ quantity pale yellow Royal Icing (see pages 20–21)

6 pale yellow carnations (see page 37)

Step 4

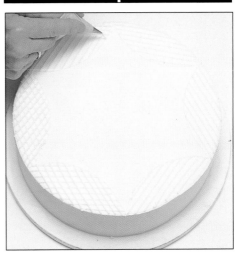

Step 3

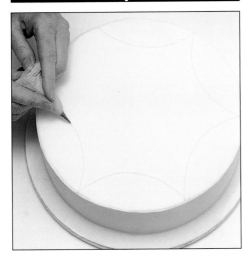

Step 7

1 Cover the cake with 3 layers of white royal icing (see page 24–25). Allow the icing to dry between each coat. Then ice the cake board (see page 85).

2 Cut a piece of baking parchment the size of the top of the cake. Fold in half to make a semicircle. Fold one side two thirds of the way across, then fold over again to make a cornet shape. Crease the edges well. Using a glass or compass, draw a concave scallop shape on the paper, making it about 5 cm/2 inches deep in the centre of the curve. Prick along the scallop line with a pin right through the paper. Open out the paper and secure to the top of the cake with

pins, then prick along the scallop shapes right through the paper to mark the icing.

3 Using a No. 2 writing nozzle (tip), outline the design in white royal icing, covering the pin marks completely.

4 Pipe a trellis (see page 33) in each scallop and leave to dry. Pipe over the trellis, using a No. 1 nozzle (tip) and yellow royal icing. Using a No. 44 star nozzle (tip), pipe a star border in yellow royal icing around the bottom edge of the cake. Pipe similar borders along the top of the cake and along the edge of the board.

5 Using a No. 2 writing nozzle (tip) and white icing, pipe loops around the side of the cake to match those on the top. Pipe a second line inside the scallop.

6 Pipe '21' on the cake, using white royal icing and a No. 2 writing nozzle (tip). When dry, overpipe with yellow royal icing, using a No. 1 nozzle (tip).

7 Fix the carnations between the loops on the side of the cake, securing with a little royal icing. Using the same nozzle (tip), pipe dots below the loops on the side of the cake.

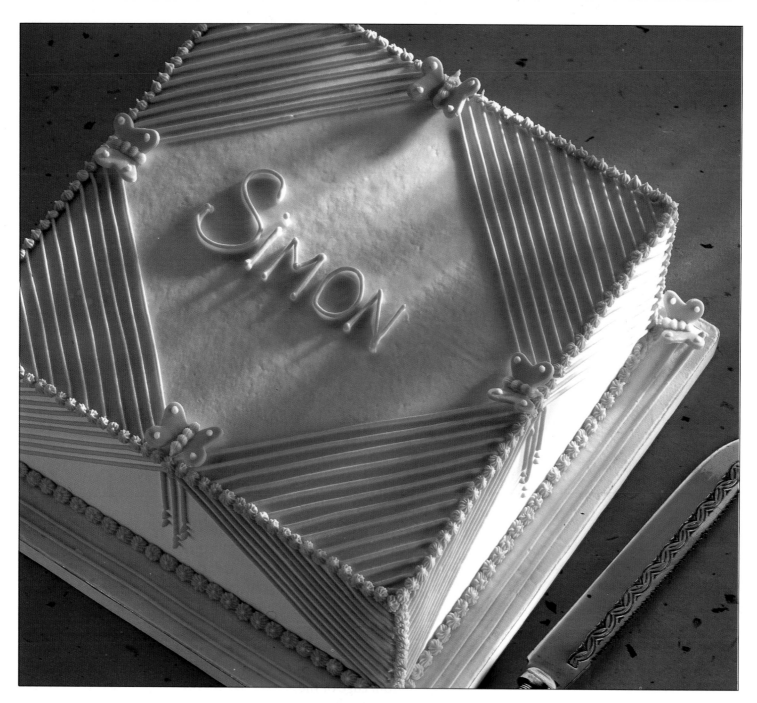

Butterfly Christening Cake

Once you have mastered the art of piping straight lines, this is one
of the easiest cakes to decorate.

Information	Equipment
No. of Servings: 20–24	square cake board
Advance Preparation: 1 day	straight pin for marking
Level of Difficulty: ✶	piping bag
	writing nozzles (tips)
	star nozzle (tip)
	butterfly cutters
	foam sponge

1 Cover the cake with 3 layers of royal icing (see pages 24–25). Allow the icing to dry between each coat. Then ice the cake board (see page 85).

2 Mark the centre point of each side on the top of the cake. Join by marking a line with a pin to make a diamond shape.

3 Use the same procedure on the sides of the cake, from the centre of each side to each corner.

4 Fit a piping bag with a No. 2 writing nozzle (tip). Half-fill with blue icing and pipe lines (see pages 32–33) to cover the pin marks.

INGREDIENTS

20 cm/8 inch square Rich Fruit Cake (see page 12)

2 quantities Royal Icing (see pages 20–21)

$\frac{1}{2}$ quantity blue Royal Icing (see pages 20–21)

8 blue butterflies (see below)

SIMPLER DESIGN

To make the cake even simpler you could leave the piping off the sides of the cake and tie a pale blue ribbon around it to match the blue icing.

5 Fill in each triangle with blue lines piped on the top and sides.

6 Pipe decorative lines (see pages 32–33) on the sides of the cake at the meeting point of the triangles and pipe a name on top of the cake.

7 Using blue icing and a No. 44 star nozzle (tip), pipe a border around the bottom edge of the cake. Finally attach the butterflies with a dab of royal icing.

TO MAKE BUTTERFLIES

1 Roll out a little blue sugarpaste (see pages 20–21) thinly and use a butterfly cutter to cut out shapes.

2 Place the butterflies on a piece of foam sponge and use the back of a knife to press the centres to give three-dimensional shape.

3 Leave to dry overnight, then decorate with a different colour of icing (frosting), using a small writing nozzle (tip).

Step 5

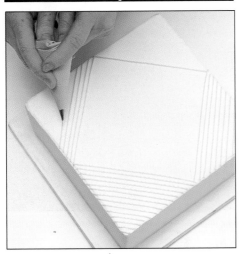

Step 6

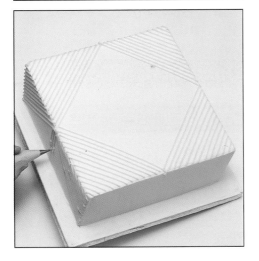

Step 7

Butterflies

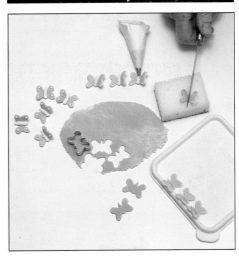

Anniversary Cake

This design may look very intricate and complicated but the pattern is really random - the only rule is that none of the lacy lines should touch each other. This cake can be adapted for a Golden Wedding anniversary by piping the decoration in yellow icing (frosting) instead of peach.

Information	Equipment
No. of Servings: 12 for the Madeira (Pound) cake; 24 for a fruit cake	square cake board
	stiff paper
Level of Difficulty: ★ ★ ★	piping bag
Advance Preparation: 3 days	writing nozzles (tips)
	small star nozzle (tip)

Step 2

Step 4

INGREDIENTS

20 cm/8 inch square
Rich Fruit Cake or Madeira
(Pound) Cake (see pages
12–14)

6 tbsp apricot jam, sieved
(strained)

1 quantity Marzipan (see
pages 28-29)

700 g/1½ lb Sugarpaste (see
pages 20–21)

1 quantity Royal Icing (see
pages 20–21)

liquid or paste food
colourings in tangerine or
orange and pink

narrow peach ribbon

about 10 pale peach moulded
leaves, 2–3 large peach
moulded roses and about 20
small peach moulded roses
(see pages 36–37)

Step 5

Step 6

1 Stand the cake upside-down on a cake board. Brush with the jam and cover with the marzipan, as described on pages 28–29. Leave to dry for 2-3 days. Roll out almost 600 g/ ¼ lb sugarpaste and use to cover the cake evenly, attaching with jam. Leave for 24 hours.

2 Cut a square of stiff paper 7.5 cm/3 inches smaller than the top of the cake. Fold it in quarters. Draw then cut out 3 convex arcs so when opened there are 4 deep ovals and 4 shallow ones. Place the template centrally on the top of the cake. Using white royal icing and a No. 2 writing nozzle, outline the template. Pipe a second outline ouside the first. Leave to dry.

3 Now make the side template. Cut a piece of stiff paper to the length of one side of the cake and 5 cm/2 inches deep. Fold in half widthwise and draw three concave arcs: the first one 2 cm/¾ inch deep; the second 1 cm/⅓ inch deep; and the third 3 cm/1⅓ inches deep. Cut out the arcs, open up the template and place against one side of the cake. Using the white royal icing and the writing nozzle, outline the template. Repeat on the other three sides, joining up the corners. Pipe a second outline inside or outside the first outline. Leave to dry.

4 Colour the remaining white royal icing pale peach by using tangerine or orange food colouring with a touch of pink. Put some of the peach icing into a piping bag fitted with a small writing nozzle

and pipe an all-over lace pattern between the side and top outlines of the cake (see pages 32–33).

5 Overpipe the white inside outline on top of the cake with the peach icing. Put some more peach icing into a piping bag fitted with a small star nozzle and pipe a border of stars all round the base of the cake. Attach the ribbon around the cake board with icing.

6 Attach one smaller rose with a stamen and a leaf to each corner of the cake with icing and then arrange the remaining flowers and leaves on top of the cake, as shown, attaching with more icing. Leave to set before serving.

Three-Tier Wedding Cake

This elaborate design uses very fine trelliswork which can be worked as either squares or diamonds. The trelliswork can be overpiped in a pastel pink to match the flowers. These roses have been tinted at the edges with pink confectioners' dusting powder (petal dust).

Information	Equipment
No. of servings: 60–80	square cake boards
Advance Preparation: 2 days	straight pin for marking
Level of Difficulty: ★ ★ ☆	piping bag
	writing and star nozzles (tips)
	8 white pillars

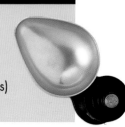

Step 3

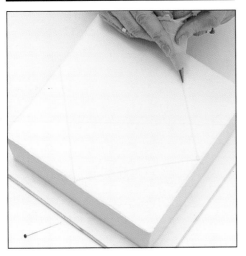

INGREDIENTS

15 cm/6 inch, 20 cm/8 inch and 25 cm/10 inch square Rich Fruit Cakes (see page 12 and 14), covered with Marzipan (see pages 28–29)

2.25k g/5 lb/20 cups Royal Icing (see pages 20–21)

5 white moulded roses (see pages 36–37)

Step 5

1 Cover the cakes with 3 layers of royal icing (see pages 24–25). Allow the icing to dry between each coat. Then ice the cake boards (see page 85).

2 Mark the centre point of each side on the top of the cakes. Join by marking a line with a pin to make a diamond shape.

3 Fit a piping bag with a No. 2 writing nozzle (tip), half-fill with white royal icing and pipe a line (see pages 32–33) to cover the pin marks.

4 Pipe a trellis (see page 33) in the 4 corners of the cakes and leave to dry.

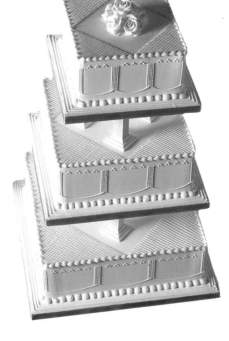

5 Using a No. 42 star nozzle (tip), neaten the edges of the trellis by piping a row of shells.

6 Using the same nozzle (tip), pipe a shell border (see page 33) at the bottom edge of each cake.

7 Using a pin, mark 2 equidistant points along each side of each cake. Using a No. 2 writing nozzle (tip), pipe 5 vertical lines from the top of the cake to within 2.5 cm/ 1 inch of the base.

8 Pipe 3 loops at the base of each set of vertical lines and a series of dots in groups of 3 along the top. Using the same writing nozzle (tip), pipe 3 parallel lines on the boards.

9 Assemble the cakes, using 8 white pillars for the structure, and arrange the moulded roses on top of the uppermost cake.

FINISHING TOUCH

Tie, or attach with dabs of royal icing, a pale pink or white ribbon around each of the cake boards.

Step 4

Step 8

INDEX